158.1
Moo

$15.00

W9-CKB-930

YOU CAN BE PRESIDENT
(Or Anything Else)

You Can Be President

(Or Anything Else)

BOB MOORE

Foreword by
MARILYN VAN DERBUR
Former Miss America

PELICAN PUBLISHING COMPANY

GRETNA 1980

Library of Congress Cataloging in Publication Data

Moore, Bob, 1934-
  You can be president.

  SUMMARY: Tells how to stop feeling inferior and
start achieving one's goals.
  1. Success. 2. Motivation (Psychology) [1. Success. 2. Motivation (Psychology)] I. Title.
BF637.S8M6   158'.1   80-36832
ISBN 0-88289-268-1

Manufactured in the United States of America

Published by Pelican Publishing Company, Inc.
1101 Monroe Street, Gretna, Louisiana 70053

Contents

To My Family

Author's Note

Appreciation to Marshall O. Donley, Jr., whose advice and assistance was invaluable in writing this book . . . and to ARSM.

Foreword

MOTIVATION! Motivation is difficult to define, more difficult to understand how to apply it to one's life for personal growth and success. Bob Moore *does both* in this book. Because I have read countless numbers of "inspirational and self-help" books I had originally planned to read only a chapter or two at a sitting but I found myself so keenly engrossed in *You Can Be President* that I read it from cover to cover without ever moving from my chair.

Since the time Bob and I met many years ago, we have kept in close touch because of our common interest and commitment—helping people to reach for and to realize their potential. He is a living example of what he has written. He truly practices what he preaches!

Bob has written a clear and concise "how-to" book, using fascinating and true examples from people's lives . . . people who owe their success story to their personal sense of motivation.

If you want to have more direction, purpose and meaning in your life . . . and all of us do . . . I wholeheartedly recommend *You Can Be President*.

MARILYN VAN DERBUR, PRESIDENT
Marilyn Van Derbur Motivational Institute
Denver, Colorado

YOU CAN BE PRESIDENT
(Or Anything Else)

Introduction

Who is Bob Moore, the author of this book?

How can he help you?

If you saw Bob Moore today, you would see a smiling, well-dressed man. He appears to be a success—and he is! He speaks to groups all over the nation, showing people how they can change their lives. He has taught and counseled thousands. And he is well paid for it.

What does Bob Moore know about being a nobody?

Bob Moore knows about being a nobody because he *was* a nobody. For years he was a nobody.

Bob Moore completed high school with a 70 average in algebra and grades not much higher in any other subject. He was a skinny kid who was laughed at in gym class.

Bob Moore started college, but only because in those days entrance exams were not given. When he received his first college report card, he had flunked three out of five courses—even though he had worked as hard as he could.

Bob Moore knew then that he was a nobody.

He gave up—dropped out of school. It was the lowest point of his life. There he was—a failure—a small young man who couldn't even pass his first college courses. He felt then the way you sometimes feel—that nothing is working out; that nothing you do is any good; that *you* are inferior, no good.

Bob Moore had quit. He had dropped out. The failure wasn't his fault (he told himself). He was sure that the cause was bad luck, or that other people were not giving him a break. Or maybe the reason was that he wasn't as rich as some people were or as big as others.

But then something changed Bob Moore. He found an idea that changed his life. He asked himself this question: "Why am I looking at what I failed to do? Why don't I look at where I have succeeded?"

Bob Moore knew that he had failed three courses. But he also knew that he had *passed* two! He had succeeded at something—he had succeeded in passing two courses. If he could pass two, he could pass more.

Bob Moore's life changed when he stopped blaming others, when he stopped looking at what was *wrong* and started looking at what was *right*. He learned that only one person could make his dreams come true. And that person was *himself*. What others were thinking, or what others did or had or said, did not matter.

Bob Moore returned to college. He never failed another course in his life. He stopped being a nobody. He became a somebody.

Bob Moore was to face more enemies. Soon after he graduated from college and was teaching, a car ran him down and smashed his legs. But Bob Moore knew he was not a nobody—he was a somebody. So he decided he would walk again and without a cane. He looked at what he *could* do, not at what he *could not* do. Today he does not even limp.

After he became a teacher and then a guidance counselor, Bob Moore discovered that he was not the only person in the world who had once thought of himself or herself as a nobody. He saw that high schools and colleges are filled with students who have low opinions of themselves—students who downgrade their abilities and their potential.

He saw that these students not only seemed to have little hope—they also did not know how to change their lives. They did not know how to start to make their dreams come true. They considered themselves hopelessly inferior. They considered themselves nobodies who were going nowhere.

Bob Moore also began to realize that many adults have the same self-doubts, the same feelings of defeat and discouragement in their lives. Bob Moore understood these feelings. As a student, he had felt like a nobody. He had felt the humiliation and embarrassment that failure brings. He had felt—perhaps as you do—that everybody else had the talent, the brains, the luck.

And Bob Moore said, "I understand. I have been there. I was once a nobody."

Years later, Bob Moore lost most of his hearing. Today he is deaf in one ear and hears poorly with the other. But Bob Moore had learned. He did not say, "This is the time to stop. This is the time to give up my dream of talking to millions of people about success and helping them become successful." He said, "I will learn to read lips. I will make the best of the limited hearing I have."

Bob Moore looked at what he *had*, not at what he had lost.

Today, Bob Moore spends his life speaking before large audiences of students and other people. He shares with them the secret he learned and learned again, the secret that can turn nobodies into somebodies.

Because Bob Moore wants to share that secret with you, he has written this book.

He will tell you how *you* can stop feeling inferior, stop being a nobody, and become a somebody.

He will tell you how to become president—PRESIDENT OF YOUR LIFE.

CHAPTER 1

Acres of Diamonds

*"I see wonderful things in people that they have not seen
or have not recognized in themselves, and I want to tell them
about these things and about their relationship to the
future."*

—Bob Moore

More than one hundred years ago in Philadelphia, six high
school seniors appealed to a man they knew—a learned
man who was a preacher—and they asked him, "Sir, would
you teach us? We would like to go to college, but we have
no money. You have degrees; you have learning. You could
teach us."

The man (his name was Russell Conwell) gave them
lessons. And he thought to himself, "If these six young men
want to learn but cannot afford college, there must be
hundreds, maybe thousands, of young people who want to
learn but who do not have the money to pay for college. I
should start a college for these young people."

So he set out to raise money for a college. In those days a
college could be built for perhaps one and a half million
dollars—not nearly as much as today, but still a consider-
able sum of money.

Russell Conwell made speeches for five years, asking
people to give money for a college that would take young
people who were not rich. After five years of speech-making,

he had collected less than a thousand dollars—not nearly a sufficient amount to build his college.

Russell Conwell was sad and depressed. When he walked to his church to write his sermon for the coming Sunday, he noticed that the grass around the church was brown and ragged. He called to the man who was hired to take care of the grass and asked, "Why doesn't this grass look better? Why doesn't it look as good as the grass in front of the other churches?"

The man who cared for the grass looked at the preacher. "Well," he replied, "I guess it doesn't look so good to you because you're comparing it to the grass across the street. It seems we always look at how good somebody else's grass looks and wish it were ours, rather than caring for our own."

Those words from the caretaker started Russell Conwell to thinking. He went into his church study and began to write a speech. The speech told how you and I spend our time looking and wishing, rather than working to make things become what we want them to be.

In this speech, he told about a man who was a farmer. The farmer owned some acres of land and made a good living from them. But the man had heard that if an acre of land had diamonds on it, a man could be wealthy beyond his dreams if he were to pick up just one handful. So the farmer sold his land and set out around the world seeking a place where diamonds could be found. The farmer traveled far and wide, to many countries. But he never found diamonds. Eventually, after 15 years, he ran out of money. One night, at the Bay of Barcelona in Spain, he killed himself.

Meanwhile, the man who had bought the farmer's land chanced to pick up a stone one day as he was out walking. When he looked at the stone, he saw that it was shiny and reflected the light. He looked closer and found that the stone was a diamond. On that very land sold by the farmer the new owner found the largest diamond mine ever discovered.

The lesson was obvious, Russell Conwell wrote. Riches are not to be found somewhere else. They come to the man who mines his own acres—who makes the most of his own land, his own abilities.

Russell Conwell gave this speech, which he called "Acres of Diamonds," for seven years. At the end of that time, he had earned eight million dollars, more than enough money to build the college he wanted.

Today, that college stands in Philadelphia, Pennsylvania. It is Temple University—built because one man saw the lesson in a simple story.

WHAT THE ACRES OF DIAMONDS STORY MEANS TO YOU

The "Acres of Diamonds" story tells one of the great secrets of life—and that secret is that *you* have acres of diamonds within yourself. The diamonds inside you are called *potential* and *ability*. There are enough of these diamonds inside you to make your dreams come true.

All you have to do is to use your "diamonds" and to pay the price to win your dream. All you have to do is to dig in your diamond mine.

How rich is your mine?

Think of this: It has been proven over and over again that most people use only ten percent of their "diamonds"—their potential and ability. Think of that—only ten percent! If you were to use just an additional ten percent of your ability and potential, you would be twice the person you are at this moment. You would be able to do twice as much, get along with other people twice as well, be twice the achiever you are!

Do you doubt that you can do this? Think: By the time you were two and a half years old, you had learned to speak the language of an entire nation! If you can learn to speak the language of a nation before you are three, think how much more you can do now.

By mining your diamond mine—by using your abilities—you can do whatever you dream of. You can become PRESIDENT OF YOUR LIFE.

CHAPTER 2

From Prisoner to All-Star

"The journey of a thousand miles begins with one step."

—Chinese proverb

This story, like all the stories in this book, is true. And, like many true stories, it tells of the difficult times that seem to come to many of us.

This is the story of a young black man. He grew up in some of the worst conditions—in a poor neighborhood in Detroit. He had little guidance except what he got from other boys he knew who avoided school, "ripped off" things, and "enjoyed" drugs.

He was arrested at age twelve—caught robbing the local A&P store. At fifteen, he was arrested trying to break into a safe in an office. Later, as an adult, he was sent to jail for taking part in an armed robbery of a neighborhood bar.

He was not a model prisoner. In fact, three times he was put into solitary confinement at the State Prison of Southern Michigan.

It was after his third time in solitary that the young man received advice that changed his life. A "lifer"—an old man who would die in prison—had seen the young man play prison baseball. "You have talent—a chance to make something of yourself," the old con told him. "Don't blow it."

The young man thought about it and made a decision. He was in prison but he suddenly understood that he had the most important kind of freedom a person can have: the freedom to choose what he would do with the rest of his life. He could choose to stop being a thug. He could choose to start being a baseball player.

Five years later that young man, Ron LeFlore, was playing center field for the Detroit Tigers in the All-Star Game! He had been given a chance by Billy Martin, who was then manager of the Detroit baseball team. Billy Martin had visited the prison during a goodwill tour. He offered the young man a tryout. Less than a year later, Ron LeFlore was playing major league baseball.

Think of it. Here was a young man at the bottom, a convicted criminal locked in jail. But he saw that real freedom, the freedom we all have, lies in the absolute power of free choice. And all of us have that power. *You* have that power.

Ron LeFlore could have said, "I have no choice. Here I am in jail. What can I choose?" But he didn't say that. He said, "I can decide. I will decide."

This free choice is the most powerful tool you have as president of your life. It is the thing that distinguishes man from the animals or from anything else that exists. You have absolute choice over your thoughts and actions, over how well or how poorly you do your work.

The world is full of people who say that choice is dead, that there is no individual freedom left. They say it is luck, rules, and laws that decide what each person must do.

This theory is not true! Victor Frankl, a world-famous psychiatrist, spent time in the German concentration camps of World War II. He studied his thoughts and talked to many other prisoners. His conclusion was, "Everything can be taken from a man but one thing: the last of the human freedoms—the freedom to choose one's attitude in any given set of circumstances—to choose one's own way."

If men and women in concentration camps have that freedom, it is clear that you who are much less confined have it too!

So you can see it is not true that we lack the freedom to choose. We can choose! The problem for most of us is that we do not *want* to choose, because when we choose we must assume the responsibility for our choices. That is the reason when we make poor choices we are quick to blame others or to say it was bad luck that kept our plans from working out. But in order to succeed, we must choose. We must exercise our freedom of choice. As president of your life you are making free choices every hour of the day.

You have the choice:

You may belittle yourself, **OR** you may be honest with yourself.

You may feel inferior, **OR** you may feel worthy.

You may put things off, **OR** you may get them done now.

You may worry and complain, **OR** you may calmly act.

You may live by the Golden Rule, **OR** you may live for yourself only.

You may think negative thoughts, **OR** you may live a life of positive thoughts and actions.

You may choose evil or good. You may destroy, or you may build. You may become what and who you want to be, or you may remain where you are. You may stick to the tasks of your life, or you may quit.

The choice is up to you.

YOU are the PRESIDENT OF YOUR LIFE.

CHAPTER 3

Cause and Effect

"Who you are will always be consistent with who you think you are!"

Daniel C. Steere

The Reverend Bob Richards is a successful man. Before he began his religious work, he was an athlete—an Olympic Champion.

How did Bob Richards achieve? He became champion by *deciding to try* and then by *practicing*. At an early age he learned that what you think and what you decide determine what you become.

At the age of thirteen, Bob Richards decided to become an outstanding athlete. He chose to learn pole vaulting. He practiced pole vaulting more than 10,000 hours. Imagine—10,000 hours of practice! Bob Richards had learned one of the secrets of success: *What you think—what you decide to do—you can do.*

"But," you may argue, "Richards was a healthy, strong fellow—he had what it took. That's why he achieved." Nonsense! *Anyone* who sets goals will achieve if he or she works hard enough.

Let's look at another athlete—one who did not have the strong body that Bob Richards had. This athlete was born with only half a right foot and a deformed right hand. But

23

from his early days as a child, his parents helped him believe: "I can do things, I can achieve."

When other boys joined the Boy Scouts and marched ten miles, this boy, with his handicaps, marched with them. He decided that he could participate. When he was a young man, he decided he would play football. He practiced constantly; he learned to make up for his deformed limbs. Then he applied to a professional football team for a position! The coach of the New Orleans Saints tried to discourage him, but he begged for a tryout as a kicker. Imagine—a kicker with half a foot! They let him try and he surprised them. He could kick a field goal 55 yards. They let him play in a few exhibition games, and he did well. As the regular season progressed, he performed better, scoring 99 points in one year. But his test came in a crucial game. The Saints were losing by one point—a field goal would win the game. Just a few seconds remained, and the team was not even at the 50-yard line. The coach said, "Okay, Tom Dempsey, go in and kick a field goal." The attempt was from 63 yards out. Dempsey went on the field and kicked the ball. It sailed straight, but would it top the bar? It did, by inches, and the Saints won the game 19 to 17. A record kick by a man who had half a foot!

Both these men—Tom Dempsey and Bob Richards—had learned that a person can do what he or she decides to do.

A UNIVERSAL LAW

This rule—that what you think is what you become—is a universal law of power. It is called Cause and Effect. It means that what you cause to happen in your mind will also happen in the physical world.

Nothing happens in this world by chance. Every happening is caused by something. To you, this means that every thought you have, every action you take, determines what will follow. If you think you can do something, if you are willing to work to achieve it, it will happen! It will happen even if you have handicaps that you think at first will stand in your way.

Let me tell you about another man who decided he would achieve.

Jim Brunotte was born a "blue baby." That meant the doctors had to change all of the blood in his body before he could live.

When he was six, he contracted polio. The doctors told him he would never walk again.

"That's ridiculous," the boy thought. He decided he wanted to walk. He began exercises and soon was walking again.

Jim Brunotte loved to ride horses. The doctors told him that curvature of the spine, a result of the polio, would make it impossible for him to ride.

Again, Jim Brunotte decided what he wanted to do. He knew about the Law of Cause and Effect. He said, "I want to ride," and he sneaked out of the hospital each weekend and practiced riding. He became a skilled rider.

In 1968, Jim Brunotte was a soldier in Vietnam. One day, the jeep in which he was riding with another soldier drove over a land mine—thirty-five pounds of dynamite. He awoke in a hospital with both legs and one arm missing. He told the attending nurse that he wanted to sit up. She said he could not. "Don't tell me that I can't," he declared.

Today, Jim Brunotte swims, bobsleds, skis, scuba dives—and he rides horses again. Using a wheelchair and other equipment, such as a saddle he invented for handicapped horse riders, he lives a full life.

Jim Brunotte and his wife run a ranch for handicapped children. It is a nonprofit business because he wants to share his abilities with other handicapped people who have not yet learned the secret of the Law of Cause and Effect.

Jim Brunotte has won awards as the Outstanding Disabled American Veteran of California and as Mr. Handicap California.

Jim Brunotte knows that what you *decide* to do, you *can* do.

Of course, the Law of Cause and Effect also means that if you say to yourself, "I can't do this" or "I don't know how" or "I won't even try," this means *for certain* that you will not succeed.

You can prove this Law of Cause and Effect to yourself this day.

Try this experiment: Go into your school, your workplace, or your home and smile at everyone you see. Think happy thoughts. Say, "Hello, I'm glad to see you!" to everyone you see. Do this for an hour or so. What is the result? It is that others smile back at you. They say "Hi! Glad to see you, too." And if you ask them to help you with something, they are ready to act.

Now try the second part of the experiment. Go to another place and act rude. Ignore people. Don't answer them when they talk to you. Say "Get out of my way" when people are near you. What is the result? It is that everyone snarls back at you. They don't smile. They tell you to get out of *their* way. If you ask them to help you with something, they probably won't even answer you.

What made the difference? Were the people different, or was it the way you thought and acted?

Ask yourself before doing or saying something, "What will be the effect? Is this what I want it to be?"

This principle is what the Law of Cause and Effect involves. It is true and real. And you can use it to achieve what you want. You can make it work for you.

By using the Law of Cause and Effect you can:
   —learn faster and better
   —become better at a sport
   —get along with others better (our experiment proved that)
   —do a better job
   —be more and do more than you ever thought you could!

The Law of Cause and Effect can help you become **PRESIDENT OF YOUR LIFE.**

CHAPTER 4

The Land Is There

"All things are possible to him who believes."

Mark 9:23

In 1952, Florence Chadwick was swimming from Catalina Island toward the California coast, attempting to set a record. She was a well-known swimmer, a woman who swam the English Channel two years before.

As she approached the California coast this day, however, she was bitterly cold. The sea was 48 degrees and she had been in it nearly sixteen hours. The fog was so heavy she could barely see the boats accompanying her.

Florence Chadwick called her friends in the boats: "Pull me out!" The people in the boats asked her not to surrender to her discomfort. "It's only a mile farther," they assured her.

In the fog she could not see the coast. She did not believe them. "Pull me out," she demanded.

They pulled her cold, wet body from the sea.

Later she told a reporter that, while she didn't want to make excuses, she thought now that she could have made it if only she could have seen the land. She had been kept from her goal by the fog.

Still later, though, she decided that it wasn't really the

fog that had defeated her. It was her own doubts. She had let the fog blind her eyes and her heart. She gave up her belief and then the fog defeated her.

Two months later, Florence Chadwick tried again to swim from Catalina Island to the California coast. Again, heavy fog rolled about her as she swam and the sea was very cold. She could not see the land. But this time she continued because, she said, she knew land was ahead of her even though she couldn't see it. She kept going toward the land she knew was there.

Florence Chadwick had learned the importance of faith and belief. She set a goal and learned to believe in it.

You, too, can set a goal. You can achieve a dream. But you must believe in it and in yourself.

Don't let the fog blind you. Don't let the fog defeat you. Your fog may not be a fog that is hovering over the California coast. But your fog can roll in on you.

Self-doubt—the opposite of belief—can make you stop swimming. It can make you get out of the water before you reach your goal—perhaps just short of your goal!

BELIEF IS A POWERFUL TOOL

Belief is a powerful tool that can help you make the Law of Cause and Effect work for you. *Cause and Effect Plus Belief Equals Personal Power!*

Belief is the magic power that makes all religions and all big ideas work. It is the power that lets people accomplish feats which would be impossible if they did not believe.

Let me give you another example of how powerful belief is.

Belief is so strong that even if *you* don't believe something, but *someone else* believes it about you, even then it works!

This is the story of an experiment that was tried and tested. An educator decided to see how much difference is made to students' grades in school if the teacher believed in the

students. Would the students who were believed in get
better grades, earn more "A's"?

The experiment worked like this: The educator told a
group of teachers that they would all have new students this
year. Some teachers were told that they would get only the
very best students—ones who could learn easily and make
good grades. Other teachers were told that the pupils
they would have were, sadly, very poor learners—they
would probably not do very well.

What the teachers didn't know was that the students were
sent to the classes by pure chance! Some good students and
some poor students were in every class.

What happened? The force of the teachers' belief about
what they had been told regarding the students was so
strong that in every instance the teachers who were told they
had poor pupils found that they indeed had them! And the
teachers who were told they had the best pupils found that,
sure enough, their students learned very well.

What a lesson about belief! It proves that when someone
believes something, really believes it, he will work to
accomplish what he believes. He will call upon his mind
and body to accomplish what he believes can be done.

And, of course, it proves the opposite, too. If you believe
you *cannot* achieve, then you *will not*. Like Florence
Chadwick on her first try off the coast of California, you
will be pulled from the water before you reach your goal.

If you believe that man can walk on the moon and put
action behind that belief—as Werner von Braun did—then
man will walk there.

If you believe you can complete a task—as Florence
Chadwick did on her second try—then you will finish it.

Sometimes our belief in ourselves leads us in new direc-
tions—even to new miracles.

The belief that Jill Kinmont had in herself changed the
direction of her whole life. In 1955, Jill Kinmont was 18.
She was the most glamorous and most publicized young

skier in America. Her picture was on the cover of *Sports Illustrated.* Jill Kinmont had faith in herself and she worked to perfect her skiing skills. She was practicing for the Olympic tryouts, and everyone believed she would succeed.

Her goal in life was to win an Olympic gold medal. Then, in the first month of 1955, a tragic accident destroyed her chances forever. In the last qualifying race before the Olympic tryouts, Jill Kinmont raced down snow-covered Rustler Mountain near Salt Lake City. The snow was faster than she expected that day and suddenly, a few seconds late on her timing for a jump, Jill Kinmont lost control and crashed into the side of the hill. She slid, tumbled, and spun down the mountain, turning somersaults in the cold.

When she came to a halt, Jill Kinmont was permanently paralyzed from her shoulders down—a quadraplegic for life. But she was alive. And Jill Kinmont knew that all people who are alive have two free choices—either to look up or to look down. She chose to look up. She chose to hold onto the belief she had in herself. She began to work to turn her new life from one of total helplessness to one of useful service. She spent days, weeks, months, and years in hospitals, surgery, physical therapy, and wheelchairs. She had good days and she had bad days. But she didn't give up her search for a life with meaning.

After years of effort, she learned to write, to type, to operate her own wheelchair, to balance her food on a special spoon that allowed her to feed herself.

She enrolled in some courses at the University of California at Los Angeles with the hope of running a ski shop. It wasn't long before she knew that it wasn't work in a ski shop that she wanted—she wanted to be a teacher.

A teacher! But she couldn't walk, and she had no training as a teacher. She got an appointment at the College of Education. After interviews with counselors, deans, and school physicians, she was told that she could never be a teacher. One of their rules for being admitted was the ability to walk up steps and stand before a classroom. She was turned down.

But Jill Kinmont now had a new belief—a belief that she could become a teacher.

In 1963, she convinced the College of Education at the University of Washington to give her a chance. She did well in her classes. And soon she was accepted for student teaching. She found that she worked well with students who seemed to have little interest—the ones who didn't seem to care. "Everyone cares—they just show their caring in different ways," she told a fellow student teacher.

Jill Kinmont earned her credentials and began to teach reading. She loved it and her students loved her. Both she and they learned and grew.

Then her father died. The family had to move back to California where she was not certified to teach.

She applied to Los Angeles school officials. As soon as they heard that she was a "cripple," they turned her down. But, as you know by now, Jill Kinmont was not someone to give up. She decided to apply at every one of the ninety school districts in the Los Angeles area. She applied to eighteen, and three wanted to hire her! The problem of access to the school was solved when ramps were built to allow her wheelchair access. Minor rules such as standing before classes were waived.

Since that year, Jill Kinmont has been teaching. In the summer she visits Indian reservations to teach remedial reading.

Many years have come and gone for Jill Kinmont since 1955. And she has never won her Olympic Gold Medal for skiing.

But she has won a gold medal—just ask her students. She won it for her teaching.

WHAT DO YOU BELIEVE?

Like Jill Kinmont, like Florence Chadwick, like hundreds of others you have heard about—you, too, can succeed if you believe in yourself. The strength of belief is amazing. A child learns to walk because his parents believe he will walk. So they make the effort to teach him—and he walks! Teachers believe that students can learn. So they make the effort to teach them—and students learn! When two people believe in marriage—believe that it can be a way for a man and a woman to be happy and successful—they work at that marriage. And the marriage succeeds! Anytime you believe in yourself and in a goal—and when you act on your belief—then you will make it happen!

Think about *your* beliefs.

What do you believe about

          —your work?

          —your future?

          —your spiritual life?

          —your self?

Are your beliefs good, strong beliefs that say, "Yes, I can" and "Others are important"? Or are they weak and negative beliefs that say, "I don't think I'm up to it"?

You have the free choice to pick whatever thoughts you want to comprise the beliefs you need and want.

Free choice—the Law of Cause and Effect.

Belief—with action behind it.

Put them together, pay the price, and you have personal power to achieve.

It's up to you.

You can be PRESIDENT OF YOUR LIFE.

CHAPTER 5

Mastering More Powers

Stop a minute and think about what you have read thus far in this book.

First you read about the "Acres of Diamonds"—about the abilities you have within yourself to make your dreams come true. You can get what you want from life by mining your own potential—your own diamond mine of abilities.

Then you read about free choice—about the freedom to choose what to do with your life. Like Ron LeFlore, the struggling young man who became an all-star baseball player, you, too, can change your life by making your own choice. You can choose to do, to work, to win.

You read about the Law of Cause and Effect. It tells you that what you think you will become is what will happen. This is a law of nature, and it is true. Everything that happens is caused by something, and if you want things to happen for you, you must first think about them—about what results your actions and thoughts will bring.

Then you learned the importance of belief—of believing in yourself and in what you can do. You learned that Cause and Effect Plus Belief Equals the Power to Achieve.

33

There is more that you need to know. There are more powers you need to master.

These powers are:

The Power of Forming Habits.

The Power of Saying "Yes, I can."

The Power of Picturing the Future.

Spiritual Power.

CHAPTER 6

Habit-Building

"Success and failure are largely the results of habit."

—Napoleon Hill

When Jimmy Carter was a schoolboy in Georgia, he wrote a school paper entitled "Healthy Mental Habits." Here is what it said:

"There are certain habits of thinking which have a good effect upon health. If you think in the right way, you'll develop:

1. The habit of expecting to accomplish what you attempt.
2. The habit of expecting to like other people and to have them like you.
3. The habit of deciding quickly what you want to do and doing it.
4. The habit of 'sticking to it.'
5. The habit of welcoming fearlessly all wholesome ideas and experiences.
6. A person who wants to build good mental habits should avoid the idle daydream; should give up worry and anger, hatred and envy, should neither fear nor be ashamed of anything that is honest or purposeful."

Men and women who know President Carter today say that these habits are still with him—still habits upon which he builds his life.

You probably know athletes who practice every day. They practice running, tackling, throwing, sliding—all kinds of skills. They perform this physical practice because they want to develop their skills to the point that they become habits—ways of doing things regularly and automatically, without having to think about them.

A good athlete learns many good habits. And he profits by them. The exercise he practices helps him days and weeks later during a game.

Musicians build habits, too. Have you ever heard a pianist practicing and practicing his scales? A typist practices, too, building over and over the habits that make the skill possible.

Driving a car is mainly a matter of building good habits—and it is particularly important because the correct response in an emergency can avoid a dangerous accident.

For an athlete, building habits is the only sure road to success. Every football player, every baseball pitcher, every basketball star will give you the same advice: "You get there by building good habits. By practicing until you do it right *automatically.*"

Nadia Comaneci, the Romanian Olympic star, is a good example of this truth. Nadia began practicing the skills of tumbling, climbing, and riding the parallel bars when she was in kindergarten! She practiced three or four hours every day. She established habits that would make her a champion.

And then it happened! Before an audience of 18,000 hushed spectators, Nadia Comaneci did what no other athlete had ever accomplished in the history of this ancient sport. She stood, poised on a sixteen-and-a-half-foot-long beam, four feet above the gym floor. Then, light and sure, she leaped into the air, flipped, and turned. She bounced from the beam with the form she had practiced during all those young years.

As the audience watched, the Olympic judges scored her performance. It was *perfect!* It was the first time in Olympic history anyone had ever earned a perfect score in that event. Nadia Comaneci smiled, with tears in her eyes. Her practice—her building habits—had carried her to victory.

What is true of *physical* habit-building is also true of *mental* exercise. A person can learn *actions of the mind* that will automatically help him in his life. These actions build habits.

You can learn to build habits of the mind—habits that will emerge automatically without your thinking about them; habits that will become a part of you and help you become the person you want to be.

HOW ARE HABITS FORMED?

Habits begin as thoughts. When you ponder something over and over and begin to act upon that thought, then the action becomes a habit.

And, of course, you can form *good* habits and *bad* habits.

We all know people who have formed bad habits. Smoking. Drinking. Taking drugs. Cursing. Being lazy. All bad habits. All easy to build.

A person smokes one cigarette. His buddies say, "Oh, aren't you smart!" So, even though he hates the taste and smell of the cigarette, he smokes another. Soon he has developed a habit of smoking. The same is true of drinking, cursing, and loafing.

Sadly, breaking habits is about twice as hard as forming them. That is the reason it is important for you to begin to form good habits now. The more good habits you start, the sooner you can be on the way to becoming what you want to be. And here is good news—it is no harder to form good habits than bad ones! A habit, once formed, will continue to work for you or against you. It depends on how good or bad the habit is.

How do you build a good habit? Let's take a small, but important, example. Let's suppose that one of the problems you have is that you do not seem to get the positive, warm response from others that you would like to get. Each time you go to work, to school, to meet people, they don't seem kind and warm to you. You want them to be, of course.

The habit you want to build, then, is a habit of *courtesy*. You want people to smile and respond kindly to you. The way to do that—the habit to develop—is this: Always say "Hello" and "How are you?" to every person you meet each day.

This habit is simple to begin. And you will be surprised how quickly people will respond to you. Just smile and say "Hello" to each classmate next to you, each person you meet on the job. It is as easy to learn this habit as it is to ignore other people or to frown at them.

And what will happen when you build this habit? An amazing thing. Remember our experiment earlier when you tried smiling and being cheerful one time and then growling another? What happened? You remember—when you were cheerful, other people smiled back at you and were helpful to you. If you make that kind of act your *habit*, then you will *automatically* get a positive response from other people.

Other good habits that you can practice are: Doing things promptly (don't put things off); being positive about an idea that is suggested (don't say, "I'm not sure that will work"); smiling even when others frown (don't let the bad habits others have bother *you*).

The secret of good habits is consciously thinking happy and positive thoughts. The person who thinks sour and sad thoughts will form negative habits. The person who thinks good and happy thoughts (you!) will form positive and helpful habits.

Don't let your habits keep you from becoming what you want to be. Don't let negative habits destroy your goals. Remember that every day we are forming and building habits. Whether we form habits that help us or habits that get in the way of our success is up to each of us.

You form and repeat habits each day. *You* can change

those habits and make them work for you. Substitute a *desired* habit for an *undesired* one.

One more hint: Habits are something to examine and to work on daily. They build slowly but surely. They can be built only day by day. They can be changed only day by day.

Check your habits now. Which habits do you have that are helping you to become the person you want to be? Which habits do you have that are *blocking you* from attaining your goals? Begin today to change these harmful habits. Begin today to build new good habits.

A word of advice: Don't try to break all your bad or negative habits at once. Don't try to build all the good habits you want at one time. Habit-breaking and habit-building take time. Work with your habits *one at a time.* But *begin* today.

And remember: The habits you build can help move you toward becoming PRESIDENT OF YOUR LIFE!

CHAPTER 7

If You Think You Can . . .

"Day by day in every way I am becoming better and better."

—Norman Vincent Peale

We have all seen Western movies. But have you ever noticed how the cowboys tie up their horses?

Here comes the cowboy down the street on his strong, white horse. He pulls up in front of the saloon where the bad guys are hiding. He leaps from his horse and wraps the reins around a railing and goes inside.

Now let us stop and think a minute. Here is a horse—a strong, powerful animal, weighing hundreds of pounds. But when the thin leather reins are wrapped around a wooden rail, the horse does not pull loose and run away; he stands in place. Why?

The answer is that the horse was trained when it was a young animal. It was tied to a post firmly, and it learned that it could not get free. It could not do what it wanted—it could only stand tied in place. So today it never even pulls on the reins.

Are *you* like the cowboy's horse? Do you stand in place because you believe that you cannot succeed—that you cannot do what you want? Suppose you pulled at the reins that held you back. Would they give way? Would you be free to act as you want?

We are all victims of suggestion. If a teacher or someone else once told us we could not succeed, we tend to believe them. And often we don't even try to succeed after that. Because we have failed once or twice, we often believe the negative suggestions that we give ourselves.

But there are tools you can learn that will allow you to pull your reins from the post and become the person you were meant to be.

These tools are called *belief in self*, or *affirmation*.

You can build belief in yourself. *You* can decide— affirm—that you are somebody, that you will do more and better this day than you did yesterday.

Forget what some person told you long ago. Forget that some *one* person *once* said you could not succeed. For one thing, he may have been wrong. And, for another, you may have changed. You can do today what you could not do yesterday.

Let me tell you about a man who learned how to succeed—and who learned it *twice*. This man came from a world of cotton fields and hot blazing sun. Hard work from sunup to sundown was his lot as a boy. He never could play sports in school because there was always work to do on the family farm. As soon as he graduated from high school, he joined the army to get away. Soon the army sent him to Germany, and it was there, in an army store, that he bought his first guitar. You see, this man had a dream—a dream that began when he first heard music on the radio his father bought for the family. He wanted to become a singer.

Once in church he heard a singing group, and he saw that after the service some people asked the singer to sign autographs. That was what he wanted, he decided—to sing so well that people would ask him for his autograph.

He taught himself to play the guitar in Germany and he

began to practice his singing, even writing some of his own songs.

After his tour of duty in the army, he tried to work toward his goal of becoming a singer, but he found no success. He was turned down for singing jobs and turned down for jobs as a disc jockey at radio stations.

He made a living selling appliances door to door. But he continued to practice his singing. He formed a small singing group that went from church to church, from small town to small town, to entertain audiences.

Finally, a recording he made started him on the way to musical history. He began drawing audiences of 20,000 or more people. Money, awards, national TV appearances—it was all his. He had believed in himself and he had won. His name—I'm sure you know it—is Johnny Cash.

But Johnny Cash was going to be tested a second time. After a few years of travel, days on the road with demanding audiences, he gave in to his weariness and began taking sleeping pills to rest, then "uppers" to keep going the next day. He began building bad habits—too much liquor, barbiturates, amphetamines. His habits became so strong he even tried to break into drugstores to get the pills he needed. He began to lose his audiences. He was no longer winning awards. His friends tried to help him, to persuade him that how a person lives speaks louder than any song. But he wouldn't listen to them. His habit became stronger. He lost control of his life.

Instead of appearing on stages he began appearing in jail cells, many of them. By 1967, he was taking over 100 pills each day.

One morning, as he was released from a jail in Georgia, a sheriff said, "Johnny Cash, I'm going to give back your money and your dope because you know better than most people that God gave you a free will to do with yourself whatever you want to do. Here are your money and your pills. Now you can throw the pills away, or you can take them and go ahead and kill yourself. Decide which one you want to do."

Johnny Cash decided he wanted to live. He decided once more that he could believe in himself, that he could succeed again. He returned to Nashville and went to his family doctor. The doctor had little confidence in him. He didn't think he was going to kick his habit of taking dope. "Only you can do it," the doctor told Johnny Cash, "and it would be a lot easier if you let God help you."

Johnny Cash began his battle. Surrounding himself with people who loved him, he locked himself into his bedroom to quit "cold turkey." The torture was great; the night-mares constant. He said later that he would doze off and imagine that glass balls were swelling up inside him, bursting and sending slivers of glass throughout his entire body. The craving for pills was still there, as great as ever. But his goal was still there, too. And his belief in himself.

After a few weeks, he started to feel human again. He could sleep without nightmares. He was making it. In a few months he was back on the stage, singing again. And he hasn't stopped. He became again the superstar he believed he was.

A few years ago, he was invited to sing at the White House before the President of the United States. It was one of the finest moments of his life. And he had done it because his belief in himself made him strong enough to succeed— twice.

You can succeed as Johnny Cash did.

This day is the beginning of a new day. Do not let what happened yesterday—or what someone said yesterday— affect what you will do today.

Today you will form new habits, make new decisions, set new goals. Today you will smile; you will be positive. Today you will learn new ideas, do new things.

How can you strengthen your desire to act anew—act positively? By saying to yourself: "I am me. I am not what someone *says* about me. I *can* do some things; I can learn to do more." Repeat this often during each day.

Here is another way you can build your faith in yourself. Think about some of the time-tested statements people have made to reinforce their beliefs. Here are some of them:

"Honesty is the best policy."

"It's never too late to do better."

"Those who live in glass houses should not throw stones."

"Where there's a will, there's a way."

"Nothing is impossible to a willing mind."

"To err is human, to forgive divine."

"It is better to give than to receive."

"Pride goeth before a fall."

"A penny saved is a penny earned."

"As ye sow, so shall ye reap."

"Everything must have a beginning."

"Practice makes perfect."

"In every cloud there's a silver lining."

"A man is known by the company he keeps."

"I can; I will."

Think about these famous sayings when you begin to doubt. Say them over aloud. Believe in them.

Remember my story. When I, Bob Moore, was in my first year of college, I failed three courses. But I looked *not at what I had failed to do,* but rather at *what I had succeeded in doing.* I had passed two courses. I decided that if I could pass two courses, I could pass more courses.

What thoughts do *you* have about *yourself* and about *your* future? Are they thoughts that are holding you back? Are they accurate thoughts? I'll bet they are not. If *you* look at what *you can do,* you can do more. If you can do more each day, you can succeed. You can say, "Yes, I can."

You can become PRESIDENT OF YOUR LIFE!

CHAPTER 8

Imagining Success

"Imagination is more important than knowledge."

—Albert Einstein

We have thought about Western movies with cowboys and badmen. Now I'd like you to imagine another movie. A movie about *you*! Imagine that it is five years from now. Shut your eyes, *now*, and imagine yourself *then*.

This is what I want you to see: A successful person, living in a new house, driving a new car, holding a new job, living with people with love in their hearts. Can you see it?

Fill in the details for yourself—the kind of house you would like, the kind of car you would wish to drive, the kind of job you would want, and so forth. If you can see this, you can achieve it! Because great living starts with a picture, held in your imagination, of what you would like to be.

You can build your desire for success only by first imagining it. You can set a goal of successes for yourself only by first imagining it.

This may seem silly to you. And it may seem pointless. But it is true. *You* have the power to create what you can imagine.

One of the great nations of modern times was built

45

because thousands of people were able to imagine what it would be—and they created it.

The nation, of course, is Israel, carved out of the Middle East after World War II. David Ben-Gurion, one of the nation's founders, said that he always kept a picture of the nation-to-be in his mind's eye.

"You have to have an ideal," he once told Golda Meir, the first woman Prime Minister of Israel. "The great men gave their lives to an ideal which everyone thought was crazy—and which became a reality."

Golda Meir was able to contribute so much to Israel because she, too, was able to imagine the new nation and its potential.

Golda Meir was born the daughter of a poor Jewish carpenter in Russia. Four of her brothers and one sister died in infancy because of disease brought on by poverty and malnutrition.

Golda Meir remembers being hungry all the time she was a child. She remembers her sister sometimes fainting in school because of hunger.

But when she was seventeen, Golda Meir learned of a dream called Zionism. It was a dream imagined by thousands of Jews who saw, in their minds, a nation of their own—a place where they would not be harmed because they were Jews.

Golda Meir and her husband emigrated to Palestine soon after they were married. Again, they found that they needed imagination. Instead of a country, they found a desert. At Merhavia, the *kibbutz* where they settled, the heat, the infestations of flies, and the bouts with malaria were terrifying. But they kept their dream, and they endured.

Years later, as Israel was growing into a nation, Golda Meir was to serve as its first ambassador to the Soviet Union. And, of course, later she contributed greatly to her country as prime minister. But throughout her hard life and her long service, she never forgot to dream—to keep her imagination alive. Her lifelong philosophy was that nothing is impossible. "I am an idealist," she admitted once, "but an idealist who believes that man is master of his fate." That is what you can be—an idealist who imagines the future and then becomes master of his fate.

If you can imagine yourself successful, you can be. If you can imagine yourself happy, you can be. If you can imagine yourself without some bad habit, then you can break it. Why is this true? Because picturing what you might become is a way you have in your mind of whetting your appetite for achieving. And unless you *want* to achieve, you cannot.

As we learned earlier in this book, your thought comes before your actions. What you want to *do* must first be what you *think*.

Now we add another part to that rule: What you first *imagine* can help you in *thinking* about what you want. And that in turn will lead you to *achieve* it.

One of the most imaginative persons today is Theodore Geisel. You probably don't recognize that name, but I'll bet you will recognize the name he uses to sign his children's books. It is *Dr. Seuss.*

The wild and inventive characters in the Dr. Seuss books have entertained millions of boy and girls. But when Theodore Geisel began imagining his strange critters, he had to hold on to his dream for a long time. He wrote and illustrated his first books and sent them to a potential publisher. The publisher said no.

"Dr. Seuss" didn't give up. He could imagine the success his books deserved. He sent a book to another publisher, and another. They, too, said no. In all, his work was rejected by twenty-seven publishers. But the twenty-eighth publisher said yes! And children's book history was made.

"Dr. Seuss"—Theodore Geisel—had the imagination to build his dream, and the faith to hold on to that dream.

Bob Bone, author of the best-selling *Maverick Guide to Hawaii* and *Maverick Guide to Australia*, widely acclaimed by travel writers as the best books on their subjects, submitted the manuscript for the Hawaii guide to 125 publishers before he found one who saw its potential. Most of us would have been tempted to give up long before we received 125 rejection slips, but Bob Bone held on to his dream—and eventually succeeded. His books are now read avidly by thousands of travelers every year.

So, as you can see, dreaming—using your imagination—is not a waste of time.

Everything that ever was, or will be, was once somebody's dream.

Psychologists tell us that thirty minutes a day of dreaming about the future is worthwhile. Obviously, if we do nothing but daydream, that is bad; but a little daydreaming can help produce results.

So relax and dream! Each dream helps move you closer to becoming what you want to become. Closer to becoming PRESIDENT OF YOUR LIFE.

CHAPTER 9

Using Spiritual Power

"Not my will, but Thine be done."

—Jesus

Heavyweight boxing champion Joe Frazier once said, "As important as roadwork is prayer."

Joe Frazier was a hard-working man who did all he could to win in the field he had chosen. But he knew he could not do it alone. He knew he needed something *beyond himself.* Joe Frazier had learned about the Universal Law of Spiritual Power.

Max Cleland, a veteran who lost both legs and an arm in Vietnam, is head of the U.S. Veterans' Administration. This man, who has overcome more handicaps than most of us will ever face, makes many speeches. And he closes with a prayer that includes these words: "I ask God for strength that I might achieve." Says Cleland, "I have learned over and over again a valuable lesson. There is help available from God when we need it most." Max Cleland had learned about the Universal Law of Spiritual Power.

Television personality David Hartman, who has appeared for years on *Good Morning America,* says it was his father who taught him about the Law of Spiritual Power. His father was a Methodist minister, and he said to David

Hartman one day, "God loves doers, not grumblers. Remember this, David, you are made in God's image, and so you have His power in you. Who's going to waste *that* kind of power?"

David Hartman says this lesson has helped him withstand disappointments in his life, to realize that God gives us all many, many opportunities.

David Hartman, the veteran Max Cleland, the boxer Joe Frazier—all understand the Universal Law of Spiritual Power.

This law is just as real as the Law of Gravity or the Law of Cause and Effect that we talked about earlier. This law— the Law of Spiritual Power—is stronger than all other universal laws.

This law is built on these truths:

God made you.

God loves you.

God will not forsake you.

God is a just God.

God *is* power.

A man who later became president of an African nation said this about the Law of Spiritual Power: "When God has put an impossible dream in your heart, He means to help you fulfill it."

What this means to you and me is that when we build a dream, God will help us!

This law means that you can use spiritual power to help you become PRESIDENT OF YOUR LIFE.

When you love someone, you help and comfort them. You give things to them.

God loves you. So if you need help, He will help you. If you need comfort, He will comfort you. To get His help, you must *ask*. And this *asking* is called *prayer*. "Ask and it shall be given, seek and ye shall find, knock and it shall be opened unto you," says the Book of Matthew (7:7).

Many people have not learned this Law of Spiritual Power. For many, God's help is the last to be sought. I think I know why many people don't ask for God's help. It is because they don't know *how* to call upon this power. For me, the way to learn how to ask, how to pray, is to read the *Bible*. The *Bible* is your greatest source of information about how you should conduct your life, face your problems, get things done. One of the main reasons Jesus came to earth was to provide an example of how we are to live so that we may become the people we are meant to be.

Men great and small have used spiritual power. Harry Truman, when he was President of the United States, once told Dr. Norman Vincent Peale that he found prayer a great source of comfort for him. "I come to this office each morning and I stay for long hours doing what has to be done to the best of my ability," said Harry Truman. "And when you've done the best you can, you can't do any better. So when I go to bed at night, I turn it all over to the Lord and forget it. I say, 'Lord, I did my best today. Now you please take over from here.'"

Faith in God—and that is what spiritual power is—can also help you overcome fear and build faith in yourself. This principle is what every religion teaches. There is God in each of us; God's power is part of each of us.

To help build your life—to achieve what you want—you can use the spiritual power that is in you. But remember, spiritual power is never forced upon you. You are not a robot. God made you a human being with free will. So you must *choose* to seek spiritual power.

In order to do this, you must practice daily and live with spiritual power as your constant and silent partner. It will help you in working with the Law of Cause and Effect. It will help you build proper ideas and beliefs.

Call upon this power to help you become PRESIDENT OF YOUR LIFE.

CHAPTER 10

The Enemies of Success

You know of the powers inside you that can help you make what you want of your life. These powers, used to bring about change, will make you PRESIDENT OF YOUR LIFE.

But at this point, I must warn you that there are enemies who work all the time to try to stop you from becoming president of your life. It will help you to defeat these enemies if you learn who they are.

The reason for this part of the book is to tell you about the enemies of your presidency.

The enemies are: "I Can't"; "What If I Fail?"; and "It's Hopeless."

Let's face these enemies now.

CHAPTER 11

"I Can't" Never Will

Not too long ago a boy was born in a run-down part of San Francisco. His family was quite poor. His parents separated when he was four, and his mother had to work every day to get enough money to feed the boy and three other children.

Before the youngster was six, a case of rickets so weakened his legs that he had to wear braces on them—not proper medical braces but homemade ones because his family could not afford a doctor's help. The rickets and braces left his legs bowed, his feet turned in, and his calves very skinny.

The boy joined gangs, and soon was arrested. After spending six hours in jail, he said, "I learned one thing—I never want to go back."

At this point in his life, the boy was invited to spend a day with other poor children at the home of Willie Mays, a baseball player with the San Francisco Giants. The baseball player told the boy he should work hard and use his energy in sports, not in juvenile gangs. Still the boy had no money—no chance to become anything, he thought.

But he began to work. To help bring in money for the family, he sold newspapers on street corners. He caught fish at the pier and peddled them. He unloaded freight cars in a railroad yard. He was a clerk in a store.

He played football in school. He decided to go to college. He would work his way through. He drove a truck to earn money while going to the University of Southern California and was fired because he fell asleep on the job.

But he didn't give up. He played more football, excelled in it and eventually became one of the most outstanding runners in USC's history. He was signed by a professional football team and became one of the nation's best known players with the Buffalo Bills. Today he is an actor and a businessman who is making millions of dollars. Of course, he is O.J. Simpson.

O.J. Simpson met an enemy—"I can't"—and he defeated that enemy.

O.J. Simpson faced the same problems you and I do— probably faced worse ones than most of us. But he did not say, "I'm not good enough." He did not say, "Why should I try?" He chose to try, and by trying, he won.

All of us face this enemy. We all think, "I just can't do it. I don't have the talent he has. I don't have the breaks he got."

We look at ourselves and we compare *us* as we look at *them*—the successful, rich, happy people. And we say, "I am a nobody—they are somebodies."

We think that others are born great, born successful, born lucky. We think that others are "naturally" good students or good workers, or that others just automatically have good marriages.

What we don't remember is that they, too, were once nobodies. They failed many times. Like O.J. Simpson, all *somebodies* were once *nobodies* who had to struggle, who had to work hard, who had to fight against the enemy, "I can't."

We often look at *what* they achieved, but not *how*. We
fail to look at the price they paid.

Let me tell you about a man who paid a terrific price for
victory. His name is Jim Hurtubise, and he has an outstanding record as a winning race car driver. Of course, Jim
Hurtubise didn't start out as a winning driver. He raced on
a few tracks while he was in the military service. Afterward,
he worked his way around the country, racing in any auto
competition he could enter. It was slow work with little
money. But Jim Hurtubise was not discouraged; he was
ready to pay the price to win.

After four or five years, he started winning some of the
big races. By 1964, he was one of the hottest young drivers
in the nation. His dream was coming true. But Jim
Hurtubise still had a heavy price to pay.

In 1964, at the Wisconsin State Fair Speedway, Jim
Hurtubise was racing in third place. The cars ahead of him
slowed, then crashed. He swerved to avoid them and
bounced off the wall. As his car came to a flaming halt, a
wheel from one of the other cars flew through the air and
smashed into his cockpit.

Unable to approach his car until the flames were ex-
tinguished, emergency crews frantically fought the fire.
When they finally pulled Jim Hurtubise from the smol-
dering ruins of his car, his hands were melted away, his
nose was gone, and burns covered forty percent of his body.
Doctors saved his life in a seven-hour operation. But his
hands were just claws. He would never drive a race car
again, they told him.

But Jim Hurtubise was ready again to pay the price for
achievement. He began a series of skin-graft operations. He
practiced squeezing bars with the stubs of fingers that he
still had. Sometimes the pain would be so bad, tears would
come to his eyes as he squeezed his fingers. But Jim
Hurtubise continued. "I knew I was going to come back,"
he said. "I never had any doubt."

After the final operation, Jim Hurtubise went to his farm in New York State and drove a bulldozer to put callouses back on his hands. And he kept practicing his driving.

Nine months after his accident, Jim Hurtubise was back on the track! He entered a race at the Trenton Fairgrounds. He didn't win—his car failed and had to be pulled from the race—but he was on his way back. Soon after, he came in second in a 200-mile stock car race. Then, two months later, he went back to Milwaukee—to the Wisconsin State Fair Speedway, the site of his tragic accident. He entered, he raced, and he won—by several miles—in a 250-mile competition. No one worked harder than Jim Hurtubise.

He didn't say, "I can't." He didn't use his accident as an excuse to stop trying. He said, "I will." He paid the price. And he won.

Jim Hurtubise learned what all of us should know. No one ever became a success without hard work, without overcoming problems. No one became a success because he was "born lucky" or because by magic he had "what it takes."

All of us begin even at the same starting line. If you say "I can't," you lose before you begin.

Have you been fighting the enemy "I can't" in your life? You can defeat the enemy "I can't" and instead choose to work, choose to achieve. You can be on the way to becoming PRESIDENT OF YOUR LIFE!

CHAPTER 12

What If Abe Had Quit?

Have you ever faced the enemy "What if . . ."?

This enemy makes us think, "What if I fail? What if I try but do not succeed?" This enemy would like us to give up.

Let me share a story with you about a man who defeated this enemy. In 1832, this man lost his job. This tragic happening saddened him, of course, but he decided to run for the state legislature. He wanted to serve others as a politician. He lost. Two losses in one year; bad losses.

He started his own business, but in less than a year it went bankrupt. He struggled seventeen years to pay off the bills from that failure.

He ran again for the state legislature. And this time he won! Maybe his life was turning around, he thought. "Maybe I can succeed."

The next year, 1835, he was engaged to be married. A few months before he was to marry the young woman he loved, she died. The strain on him was too much; he broke down and was in bed for months in 1836 with nervous exhaustion.

In 1838, now feeling better, he ran for the office of speaker of the state legislature. He lost. In 1843, he ran again for office—this time for the Congress of the United States. He was defeated.

Wouldn't you have given up by now? Trying and trying again and losing and losing. Business failed . . . sweetheart died . . . rejected by the voters of your state. When do you quit—give up on things that are important to you?

This man *did not* give up; he did not say "What if." In 1846, he ran for office and was elected . . . this time to Congress.

Two years later he sought renomination. He thought he had done a good job in two years of Congress. Surely the voters would give him a chance to serve again. They did not. He lost the nomination.

He was broke financially. He applied for the job of land officer in his state. His application was returned with a letter that said, in effect, "To be a land officer in this state requires someone of great talent, great ability, great intellect. Your application does not meet these qualifications."

Two more defeats. Would you have kept on trying? When would you have just said, "I am a failure"?

But this man pressed onward. In 1854, he ran for the United States Senate! Once again he lost. Two years later he ran for nomination as Vice-President of the United States. He lost. Two years after that defeat, he ran still another time for the United States Senate. He lost.

This man had made 11 tries and won just twice. When would you have given up?

But Abraham Lincoln—yes, he was the man who lost nine out of eleven tries—did not give up. He remained president of his life and in 1860, two years after his last defeat, he was elected President of the United States.

Abraham Lincoln faced the same enemies that you and I face. He did not run—he stood and he fought. He was not willing to give up; he would not quit.

Like you and me, Abraham Lincoln had a free choice. He could have turned away, but he didn't. Nor do you and I need to turn away.

Let me tell you a rule guaranteed to make you a failure. *As soon as you fail once, give up.* Don't try again. I promise you that you will never win this way.

And I will give you a rule guaranteed to make you a success. When you fail once, try again. Forgive yourself for failing.

Have you ever heard the voice of failure? The voice says, "If you fail when you try, then give up, stop, quit, walk away." The voice says, "You're a nobody."

Don't listen to that voice. Successful people don't listen. When they fail, they try again. They say to themselves, "That was one way *not* to achieve what I want. Now I'll try another way."

This approach requires starting each day with a clean slate. Begin each morning *not* by saying to yourself, "I bet I'll flunk another test, lose another job, come in last." No! Say to yourself, "Today I'll do what I can. It doesn't matter that I lost yesterday or the day before. Today is a new day. I'll try again."

When Jesus was asked, "How many times should we forgive a person, seven times?" He answered, "Seven times seventy."

If He would forgive your errors, so you must forgive yourself. Start today with a clean slate. Make today the first day of your PRESIDENCY OF YOUR LIFE.

CHAPTER 13

Lucy's Impossible Dream

O.J. Simpson—a modern athlete; Abraham Lincoln—a great American President. Did they succeed because they were "chosen"? Did they just "get the breaks"? No, they succeeded because they worked hard to overcome the same enemies that you face, the enemies that would keep you from becoming what you want to be, the enemies that would keep you from becoming PRESIDENT OF YOUR LIFE.

These enemies are "I can't," "What if I fail?" and "It's hopeless."

One of my close friends and favorite people is Marilyn Van Derbur. You may know her as a former Miss America and prominent television personality. Marilyn Van Derbur left the glamour of show business to pursue a goal. Her goal was to talk to people, especially students, about making dreams come true in their lives.

Marilyn Van Derbur has succeeded. She speaks to more than 300,000 people each year. Her films on self-direction have been viewed by literally millions of men and women, young and old. She has been named "outstanding woman speaker in America" for several years. All of those who are exposed to this great lady find that her message influences their lives in a positive way.

She tells the story of a good friend of yours and mine. It is a story that tells us a lot about overcoming the enemies that block our success. She tells about a woman born in a small town in upper New York State. When she was a very small girl, she would tell everyone she met that she was going to become one of the best-known actresses they had ever known. The neighbors and friends laughed and smiled at the little girl. They were sure her dreams were just girlish thoughts.

But she didn't forget her dream. When she was 18—with her mother's permission—she went to New York City to enroll in an outstanding acting school. For three months, she worked her heart out. She knew she was going to be a fine actess. She knew she was talented.

At the end of three months, the school sent her mother a letter. It read, "Our school has produced some of the greatest actors and actresses the United States, even the world, has ever known. However, we have never had a student with less talent and ability than your daughter. She is no longer enrolled in our school."

But this girl wasn't going to accept being kicked out of school, being told she could never be an actress, being told she was a nobody. She spent the next two years taking odd jobs in New York City—as a waitress, a hat-check girl, anything that would give her enough money to live on. Between working hours, she applied at rehearsals of plays. You don't get money for rehearsals. You get paid only if you last until the play opens. With every play she auditioned, she was called in before opening night. She was always told, "You have no talent, no ability. Get out."

After two years, she caught pneumonia. Tremendous pains racked her body, and she had to go to the charity ward of one of New York City's large hospitals, for she could not afford to pay. Three weeks after she entered the hospital, a doctor came by and told her that she probably would never walk again. The pneumonia had so weakened her legs that they were withered.

The girl, by now a young woman, had to go back to her mother's home in upper New York State.

She returned with two facts to confront: She still had her dream of becoming an actress, and she had legs on which she could not walk.

Her mother believed in her—believed she could some day walk again. Together, mother and daughter, with help from a local doctor, began a program to restore her legs. They began with 20-pound weights in each shoe and braces on both legs. She tried to walk with crutches under both arms, and she fell to the floor. Two years later, however, by painful daily practice, she was walking. She had a limp, but learned to keep it from showing.

At age 22, she returned to New York City to try again. And for the next 18 years—yes, *18 years*—she failed to become the actress she wanted to be. She was 40 years old when she got her first noteworthy acting role.

When would you have given up? When was the last time you just threw up your hands and said, "I've tried long enough. It's impossible."? Would you have tried two years? Five? Ten?

This woman finally got a chance when, at age 40, she won a television role and was on her way.

Let me tell you how successful she became. In 1953, *29 million people* watched on television as Dwight D. Eisenhower was inaugurated President of the United States. In 1953, *33 million people* watched as Elizabeth II was crowned Queen of England. In 1953, *over 40 million people* watched a woman who was a failure for years—a woman who worked 18 years without getting a good acting job.

It was Lucille Ball's television special. Few of the reviewers looked for a limp caused by early illness. All they noticed was the talent and ability of one of America's greatest actresses—a woman who defeated her enemies and became *somebody.*

Lucille Ball. Born great? Born talented? Born "I Love Lucy"? Given the breaks? No. Lucille Ball was just a person who would not give up, a person who did not say, "I can't," "What if I fail?" "It's impossible."

Lucille Ball first became president of her life. Then she became the successful person millions cheered.

You have the same free will that Lucille Ball had. The decision to stand and battle the enemies of your presidency is totally up to you. Whether or not you strike out once or twice, or even three times, and then close the book is your decision.

Remember the great Babe Ruth struck out 1,330 times! He held the world record as the strikeout king. But Babe Ruth also swung successfully many times. He hit 714 home-runs—a record that stood until Hank Aaron topped it to become America's new home-run leader. Which do you remember—Babe Ruth's strikeouts or his home runs?

If you try, you will be commended for your hits—not for your strikeouts. But you must try and try again. The choice is up to you. Only *you* can keep *you* from becoming the person you want to be. Only *you* can make the decision to become **PRESIDENT OF YOUR LIFE.**

CHAPTER 14

Your Presidential Cabinet

Now you know about the enemies of your Presidency—forces ·that would like to make you surrender control of your life. Forces that want to make you say: "I can't do it." Forces that want you to doubt yourself, to have you say: "What if I fail?" Forces that want to hear you give up and say, "It's hopeless." But your Presidency has *friends*, too.

In fact, as you build toward becoming PRESIDENT OF YOUR LIFE, you have a whole Presidential Cabinet full of forces that can help you.

Just as the President of the nation has a cabinet of friends who advise him, you have a cabinet of friends who can advise you.

These friends are:
    Enthusiasm
    Action
    The Golden Rule
    Patience
    A Positive Mental Attitude
    Goals
    Self-Confidence

These friendly forces are there for you to call upon. They are waiting to serve you—to strengthen you when you need a push, to comfort you when you begin to hear the "I can'ts" and "It's hopeless."

Learn to use your Presidential Cabinet, and you can speed your way to achieving what *you* want from your life. You can cease to be a nobody and begin to know that "I *Am* Somebody."

The next part of this book will introduce you to your Presidential Cabinet.

CHAPTER 15

Enthusiastic Dolly

When Dolly Parton was born, she was the fourth child of 12 boys and girls. She was born in a two-room wooden shack in Sevier County, Tennessee. Her father scratched a meager living from a patch of mountain soil. Dolly Parton did not start with the advantages, to say the least. Her early life was hillbilly life at the poorest—wooden shacks for homes, wringer washers for the clothes, trash and car parts in the front yard. But Dolly Parton gave herself something that meant she would not grow up to be just another mountain woman raising a herd of children. She gave herself *enthusiasm!*

When she was a toddler, she learned to sing. At age five, she was devising lyrics for songs with her mother recording the words in writing. At age seven, Dolly Parton made her own guitar from parts of old instruments. The next year, an uncle gave her a real guitar. And she continued to sing.

In high school, she didn't have pretty clothes to wear. But she had her dream. She had *enthusiasm.* One of her sisters now reflects, "Dolly wasn't shy about telling her dreams.

Where we lived in the hills, *nobody* had dreams like that; so naturally the kids laughed."

As you know, Dolly Parton has kept on singing all her life. She became the first woman ever to have a million copies of an album bought by her fans. Her enthusiasm has never stopped.

Dolly Parton's life offers you an example of how you can use *enthusiasm* to keep you going—to keep you moving toward your goals—to keep you moving until you become PRESIDENT OF YOUR LIFE.

What is enthusiasm? When you have a goal, a purpose that you believe in, when you are working to make that goal come true, then you have energy, excitement, and anticipation inside you; *then* you have enthusiasm. You feel happy and self-confident.

I don't mean that you should always smile or that you should think that circumstances are always perfect—that everything is wonderful. That isn't enthusiasm. That is being a Pollyanna, and that doesn't last very long.

No, the enthusiasm you need as a member of the Cabinet of Your Presidency is more a way of thinking and approaching things. It is a way of thinking that says to you, "Life is good. There *are* ways to succeed."

When you have enthusiasm, you don't look at the bad side of things as they happen. You look at the good. You find something good in each person, in each happening.

Real enthusiasm means you believe that what you are doing has a purpose. You have a strong conviction that you *can* accomplish your purpose, and you have a burning desire to stick to your goal until you have reached it.

One of the people who comes to my mind when I think of enthusiasm is Carol Channing, the singer, actress, and recording star. She developed her enthusiasm when she was in the fourth grade! She was called on to make a talk before her fellow students. She didn't know what to say, so she did an imitation of a well-known person in the school.

"The kids started to laugh," Carol Channing recalls. "I thought, 'My gosh, what I laugh at, everybody else laughs at. What I think is funny everybody else thinks is funny.' This is the most delicious feeling I've ever had." From that moment on, Carol Channing had a goal. "I will bleed. I will die. I will crawl. I will do anything to get back on the stage," she vowed.

Carol Channing was a success many years ago in the musical "Hello Dolly." Recently she started a nationwide tour to bring "Dolly" back. "I thought everyone was Dollyed to death," she said. But Carol Channing discovered again that if you have enthusiasm for something, you can win. Her revival of "Hello Dolly" broke records for attendance everywhere it went. "You have to have a purple passion for whatever you're doing," Carol Channing says.

You can win, too, if you develop a "purple passion" for your goals. You can have enthusiasm.

Enthusiasm means:

You look at what needs to be done and find ways to do it, rather than finding excuses for not doing it.

You find out that the more you learn about something, the more you want to know.

You do the little things of life with pleasure. Anyone can enjoy a vacation, a holiday, a new car. The enthusiastic person finds pleasure *every day*, getting done what he knows he wants to do.

You look forward to living today and tomorrow. You act calmly, you are less critical of others, you help others feel needed and appreciated.

But all of these attitudes are not the best part of having enthusiasm. The best part is this: When you have enthusiasm, you find it easy to defeat the "I can't" and "It's impossible" enemies!

When you are tempted to quit and give up, your *enthusiasm* carries you on. When thoughts of doubt, worry, and fear enter your mind, your *enthusiasm* chases them out.

Your enthusiastic belief that you can do what you want is

stronger and more powerful than any negative forces—any enemies of Your Presidency.

The enthusiastic person knows that things don't *always* go right. He knows that sometimes it will seem as if his dreams *never* will come true. But the enthusiastic person gives himself a pep talk, digs into the task at hand, and soon he is working harder than ever and feeling better than ever.

I have a secret way I use to build up my enthuriasm when it fades. I think about all the people in this world who do things—achieve goals—who started with *nothing* but became *somebody.*

I think about Dolly Parton, who sang her way into millions of hearts starting from hillbilly poverty.

I think of a salesman I heard about. This man, named Bob Patchen, sells real estate in San Mateo, California. He never finished high school, but he makes hundreds of dollars a month selling real estate. And he is blind!

I think about a man named Braz Walker who makes a good living writing books about tropical fish. He probably knows more about tropical fish than anyone in this country. At age nineteen, he became ill with polio. From that day until now, he has been flat on his back. He can breathe only with a mechanical device. He writes books with a special device that he operates by moving the only part of his body that he can control—his tongue!

I think about James Benson Irwin. After an airplane crash, he was in the hospital with two broken legs, a broken jaw, and a brain concussion that took away his memory. After two years of medical help and hypnosis to restore his memory, he was back in the cockpit of a plane. Then he applied to become an astronaut. He was turned down. Four times he applied; four times he was rejected. But Jim Irwin kept his enthusiasm—he applied again. He was accepted and became the eighth man to walk on the moon.

You can't stop a person who knows where he is going— and who has the enthusiasm to take him there. You can't defeat a person who won't be beaten. *You* cannot be beaten if *you* use Enthusiasm as a member of the Cabinet of Your Presidency.

Allow Enthusiasm to build in your life. Allow your enthusiasm to work. Allow it to charge the currents of your life. Allow Enthusiasm to help you become PRESIDENT OF YOUR LIFE.

CHAPTER 16

Do It Now

The next member of the Cabinet of Your Presidency is *Action*. Action means "Do it now."

Suppose you saw a person standing by a swimming pool looking at the water and he asked you, "How do I begin to jump?" You would answer, "Just jump. Don't think about it, do it!" This is what "Do it now" means.

Think about a powerful, modern automobile. There it stands, shining, attractive. But it won't get you or anyone else anywhere unless someone turns the key and gets it started. It may be the best and fastest car on the road, but we will never know if it doesn't get started.

That's the way it is with the goals you want to achieve. You may have the finest ideas in the world. Your goals may be excellent. But if you don't "Do it now," nothing will happen.

This is the rule: "Action comes before all results. And the amount of action equals the amount of results." Most people never get the results they want because they do not take the action that brings the results. Most people have dreams, but few people *act* to make the dreams come true.

Let me tell you about one man who acted on his dream. At one time in his life, 18 cents and two cans of sardines stood between him and starvation. He had to move often from one cheap apartment to another in Greenwich Village because he could not pay the rent. Twenty years of his life had already been spent in the U.S. Coast Guard. While working as a cook in the service he used his night hours and free time writing letters for fellow enlisted men to their girl friends—men who were illiterate and couldn't put words on paper.

During these times he fell in love with writing. He didn't know it then, but his writing was to carry him to fortune, fame, and purpose. His success was anything but instant, however. He wrote seven nights a week for eight years before he sold his first magazine article—for $100.

When he retired from the Coast Guard, he dedicated himself full-time to writing. His income was most irregular, but his bills never failed to arrive.

He was offered a job in government during these trying times, but turned it down. "I'm a writer," he said. "I've got to keep on writing."

Time passed and assignments came in more regularly, but they never came in as fast as the bills. He learned to have editorial conferences over lunch so the editors would pick up the bill.

But he had a dream, and it had become so strong that he turned it into a goal. His goal was a book that he thought would take two or three years to write. It took twelve, and almost broke him—mentally and financially. Nine years after beginning the book, this man was in debt over $100,000. Quite a price to pay for a dream.

Depression set in, and he almost gave in to it. Alone one night on a ship's deck in a darkened ocean, the only way out of it seemed to be for him simply to go overboard. But at that moment he discovered a strong feeling of belief in his book and belief that it would be of value to others. He moved away from the rail.

After twelve years of putting action behind his goal, the book was published. The rest of the story is history—1.6 million copies in hardback sold, another 3.7 million in paperback in America alone.

When the book was dramatized on television, it broke all records, attracting a viewing audience of more than 130 million people. It became the highest rated television show in history. It won nine Emmy awards and literature's coveted Pulitzer prize. His personal fortune has already passed the $5 million mark.

Roots was the name of the book and the television series. Alex Haley was the writer.

Alex Haley—a man who declares, "The only way to succeed is by hard work and faith. No magic button can guarantee instant success—you simply must believe. You must have faith—and when the going gets rough you just have to hang in there."

Alex Haley "did it now." He didn't postpone writing to take a job. He didn't "do it later"—*he began working now at what he had set as his goal.* He "just jumped."

That is what you must do. "Just jump."

If you have been an "I'll do it later" person, the only way to become a "Do it now" person is by beginning. There is no other way. Success begins with your first "Do it now."

Want to improve your physical strength? Then begin with "Do it now." Want to get along better with others? Then begin with "Do it now." Want to make more money? Then begin with "Do it now." Want to kick some bad habit? Then begin with "Do it now." Want to get better grades? Then begin with "Do it now." Got problems? Then begin to solve them with "Do it now." None of your hopes, or dreams, or goals will ever happen until you *act* on them.

Thinking about them will not make them happen. Wishing for them will not make them happen. Dreaming about them will not make them happen. They will come true only when you put *action* behind them—when you begin to mine your diamonds.

Some people don't begin to "do it now" because, they say, the timing isn't right. They want to wait for a better chance, a better opportunity.

One year recently when the Dallas Cowboys football team was not doing as well as it might have, someone suggested that the team wasn't getting the breaks—wasn't making "the big play."

One player, Tony Dorsett, was asked about that analysis. He disagreed. "We have a lot of weapons on this team," he said, "and this gives us the tendency to fall back and depend on that, maybe too much."

Tony Dorsett continued, "You can't win games sitting back waiting for the big play all the time. We have to be ready to go three yards in a cloud of dust if we have to." Tony Dorsett had learned that "Do it now" means that in order to win, you do not wait for the "big play."

And this is true for *you*, too. Do not wait for the "big break" or the best time to act. The time to act is *now*. There is no perfect time, no right energy, no full ability—these all develop by beginning. "Just jump."

Let me remind you of one other thing: Only *you* can begin for *you*. Only you can take your first step. No one can do it for you.

How often have you heard the expression, "Beginning is half the job"? That statement is true. Once you jump in, you will have started, and that start can keep you moving toward your goal.

Some people don't begin to act because it is hard work. They think they can find some other actions that are easy. Successful people never look for the easy job. The smartest, most competent people in the nation have always had to work diligently!

President Lyndon Johnson would begin his day in the White House at 6:30 a.m. and work a fourteen-hour day. Henry Kaiser, the great industrialist, scheduled his work day carefully—he even allotted exactly five hours for sleep. And he kept a pad and pencil next to his bed so he could write down ideas that came to him while he was resting! Charles Finley, the baseball owner who built the Oakland Athletics into a world championship team, has one formula: "Sweat plus sacrifice equals success." He believes in this precept so much he had it engraved on each of the World Series rings he gave his players in 1972.

Action means work, hard work. It means hard work to businessmen and to athletes. It means hard work for the President of the United States or for you as President of Your Life. But to act is to win. To act is to live fully. Don't balance on the edge. Jump in!

CHAPTER 17

The Golden Rule

The Bible says: "And as ye would that men should do to you, do ye also to them likewise." This statement appears in many religions, many philosophies. We call it the Golden Rule. It is a rule that you should add to the Cabinet of Your Presidency. It is a rule that can *help you as you help others.*

A successful person knows that he cannot do it alone. You and I live in a world full of other people. How we deal with them—how we treat them and how they react to us—is determined by how well we follow the Golden Rule. Men and women who achieve have found that the Golden Rule works for them.

Carol Burnett, the television actress, tells a fascinating story of how her life changed because of the Golden Rule.

At the time, Carol Burnett was an acting student at the University of California at Los Angeles. One of her professors had invited a group of students to entertain at a bon voyage party he was having before he left for Europe. Carol Burnett was among the students. After the performance, she was speaking with the professor. He said he admired her performance and asked what goals she had set in her life.

Carol Burnett told him she hoped to go to New York and make a career on the stage. But she admitted she didn't have enough money to get started, let alone live in New York until she could launch a career. She didn't tell him the whole story—which was that she and her mother and her grandmother had been on welfare. Money was definitely something she and her family did *not* have.

The professor said he would be happy to lend her the money to get a start in New York. One thousand dollars should be enough, he added.

It turned out that the professor was quite serious. He and his wife sat down with Carol Burnett and explained the offer in detail. Three conditions existed if she took the money, they cautioned her. First, if she did succeed, she would pay the loan back without interest in five years. Second, she was never to reveal his identity to anyone. Finally, if she accepted the offer, she was eventually to pass the kindness along to another person when she was able to do so. In other words, she was to follow the Golden Rule. Do unto others . . . .

Carol Burnett accepted the loan. She has long since paid it back. And, although she doesn't talk about it, those who know her are sure she has carried out the third condition more than once. Carol Burnett learned that none of us can do it alone. We all need help from someone.

That applies to you, too. You can go nowhere without other human beings.

We live in a world made up of other people. These people—like you and me—have a strong desire to be needed, to be liked, to be respected. If they are not needed and respected, they feel like nobodies. And a world of nobodies would be of no help to you!

As President of Your Life, you have no control over other people, over what they do and say. But you *do* have control over what *you* do and say. Are your actions towards others making them into nobodies? Or do you treat them in ways that make them feel like *somebodies?*

Your actions will always do one or the other. If you try to turn others into somebodies, you will not be alone in your actions.

I am sure you have heard of Alcoholics Anonymous. It is a group of men and women who help others afflicted with the disease of alcoholism. But did you know there are dozens of other "Anonymous" groups in our nation? There are groups for fat people (Overeaters Anonymous), for compulsive gamblers (Gamblers Anonymous), and for people with emotional problems (Emotions Anonymous).

In all, it is estimated that *five million Americans* are helping other people in such groups! And they are all doing it quietly and without seeking credit. They are all following the Golden Rule. Do unto others . . . .

Have you ever wished other people would act differently toward you? Have you ever wished others would be kinder and more considerate? Most of us have felt that way. What we sometimes forget is that *the way we are treated by others* is caused by *the way we treat them.* So if you want to bring about a change in the way others treat you, you must first change *your* behavior and actions towards them. The way to do this is to practice the Golden Rule every day you live.

Some people might think practicing the Golden Rule is square or old-fashioned. Roger Staubach, star quarterback for a champion football team, the Dallas Cowboys, is a firm believer in the Golden Rule. And he has been called "square." Says Roger Staubach, "If loving my family and being a Christian are square traits, then I'm proud to be a square."

Rober Staubach treats others as he wants them to treat him. The result? Here is what he says: "When I walk through the locker room, I sense that my teammates *respect* me. I hope to set a daily example that might make others want to pursue a firmer association with God."

Isn't this how you would like other people to think of you—with respect? Then the answer is the Golden Rule: Treat *others* with respect and they will treat *you* with respect.

We cannot make the most of life without faith in each other. This is another way of saying the Golden Rule.

The Golden Rule means:

• You think first about what *you* did wrong if you don't get along with another person before thinking what *he* did wrong.

• You don't try to build up yourself at the cost of tearing others down.

• You look for good points others have—even if they have a reputation for meanness, thoughtlessness, and lack of consideration. You will be amazed at how often what you expect of a person is what you get from him.

• You appreciate what others do for you. And you let them know you appreciate what they do by a sincere "thank you."

• You don't wait for others to be friendly—you act friendly first.

Golden Rule Presidents learn to control themselves. When they are tempted to "tell someone off," they practice silence. Silence is the very best weapon against saying things or doing things you will wish later you had not said or done.

Golden Rule Presidents "go the extra mile." They don't wait to settle differences or hurts. They "Do it now" and clear things up.

The Golden Rule is a strong tool in the Cabinet of Your Presidency. Learn to use it and it will help you get what you are wishing for.

But let me give you one reminder: Golden Rule Presidents do not act thoughtfully toward others because of what they will get out of it. The Golden Rule does not work that way.

Your actions must be honest and real; and they must seek

no reward, no payment, no applause. You cannot give the gift of yourself and your actions to others if you give only to get in return.

Remember the words of John F. Kennedy when he was inaugurated as President of the United States: "Ask not what your country can do for you, but what you can do for your country." This was another way of saying the Golden Rule.

If you think in terms of what you have to *give* rather than what you have to *get*—then you will be on your way to becoming PRESIDENT OF YOUR LIFE.

CHAPTER 18

It Takes Time

You are eager to become PRESIDENT OF YOUR LIFE.
You want to move as rapidly as you can to achieve your
goals. As you move toward your goals, though, remember
this word of caution: *Becoming a new person takes time.*

"Rome was not built in a day." I'm sure you have heard
this saying. You know, too, that great accomplishments can
take a long time. The Egyptian pyramids were not built in
a few months, but over many years. Great cathedrals
sometimes take a hundred years to complete. What this
means to you is that *you* must have *patience.*

I recently heard about an experiment that shows the
value of patience. For this experiment, a small bottle cork
was suspended by a thin silk thread. Hanging next to it was
a heavy steel bar, hung by a metal chain. The cork was set
in motion, pulled to one side so it would bump gently
against the steel bar each time it swayed back and forth. For
minutes nothing happened. The cork would bump the steel
bar and bounce away. Ten minutes passed, then twenty.
Still nothing happened to the steel bar. Then, suddenly,
after more than a half hour, the steel bar began to tremble

from the impact of the tiny cork! Each time the cork struck, the steel bar trembled more. Then the steel bar started to move just a bit, then a bit more. In another half hour, the steel bar was swinging back and forth as the cork had done. The cork, having done its work, was removed. The steel bar continued for some time to swing back and forth.

What a lesson in patience this experiment teaches us!

How many times have you thought, "I couldn't make a difference—I'm not big enough or bright enough"? But like the tiny cork, we all can move steel bars if we have patience. That is why patience is another friend you should add to the Cabinet of Your Presidency.

Patience teaches us that we must, first of all, live one day at a time. You cannot overcome all your problems in a single day. You cannot carry out all your plans in one day. You must be patient; like the tiny cork, you must take your time.

Athletes call this "pacing yourself." When a football or baseball season starts, the players do not run out on the field the first day and start playing at full speed. No, they begin practicing and exercising weeks and months before the first game. They pace themselves, doing a little more each day. And when opening day comes, they are ready to play.

Think of how a weight lifter gets to be a winner. He starts with small weights. He adds a few more pounds each day, each week. Eventually, he may lift hundreds of pounds.

This approach is the way you can use patience. Begin now—"Do it now!"—but begin one step at a time, one day at a time.

"Inch by inch, anything's a cinch," someone once said.

Nobody learns to read, to work mathematics, to play a piano, or to do anything worthwhile in one day. Nobody breaks old habits in a day. Nobody builds new habits in a day. Everyone who achieves learns to pay the price of time. And that means *patience.*

What is your patience level? Are you willing to go after your goal one step at a time, one day at a time? Of course, you get tired of working and striving and not seeing results. Sometimes it seems you will *never* get where you are headed.

I recall vividly how discouraged I became during the years I spent preparing for writing this book. One particularly low point I remember clearly. It seemed that I just couldn't fit all the material together in a concise and direct manner. I would write pages and pages about points I felt should be summarized in just a few sentences. I began to wonder if I would ever be able to complete a worthwhile manuscript, and if anyone would find it valuable should I complete it.

One day during this time of discouragement, I was in Washington, D.C., having lunch in a resturant. I was meeting with a person who was the president of a great organization, and we were discussing my speaking engagement before an upcoming convention. I spent about twenty minutes intently outlining the talk I would make. I illustrated what I was saying with examples from my proposed speech. I was so involved with the discussion I did not realize someone was at the table next to mine. But shortly before I left, the waiter brought me a note. He said a customer had left it as she paid her bill and asked him to give it to me.

Let me share it with you. It said: "Dear Sir: Forgive me for eavesdropping, but your words concerning determination and genuine effort were exactly what I needed. My goal is one some say is impossible to reach. I am more encouraged by your words than by the three days of conferences I just attended. Thanks for the inspiration." It was signed, "The Woman Who Sat Next to Your Table."

I realized then that I had allowed fear and doubts to cause my discouragement. This one note brought me back to my purpose—my goal. I knew again that the price of patience was worth paying.

Remember some of the men and women we read about earlier in this book. Think about Lucille Ball, who struggled until she was forty before she was accepted as the actress she wanted to be. Could you wait that long? Do you have the patience to reach your goals?

Think about O.J. Simpson, working his way through school, trying again and again before he succeeded.

Think about Abraham Lincoln, who failed repeatedly. Yet he was patient. He kept his goals clear in his mind and he tried. When he failed, he tried again.

This is what patience is all about.

Patience allows you to keep on because you know that if you work at something long enough and persistently enough, you will ultimately succeed. This is true about getting along with other people. This is true about learning a subject in school. This is true about getting ahead on a job. This is true about improving a marriage. The patient person succeeds. The patient person knows, too, that you must do one thing at a time. You must take each task, complete it, then go on to the next.

When you try to do too many things at one time, nothing is done properly. You become nervous and irritable. You get discouraged.

When you have a busy day—when it seems as if there are dozens of tasks that you *must* get done—this is the rule you need to remember: Do one thing at a time. This means don't watch television and read at the same time. This means make a list of the things that have to be done; then check them off your list, one at a time, as you finish them. This means staying calm. You can do whatever needs to be done if you take one thing at a time.

You can change your life to become the person you want to be *if you make the changes one at a time.* Try solving all of your problems at once and you *never* will win. Take the problems one at a time and you *always* will win.

Patience also means remembering that sometimes it takes *dozens*, maybe *hundreds* of attempts before you get it right. Remember "Dr. Seuss," who took his book to twenty-eight different publishers. Think of Thomas Edison, who failed in over 10,000 attempts to make an electric light before he succeeded.

I know of a lady who failed her driving test *one hundred and two times*. But she didn't give up. At age seventy-five, she tried the one hundred and third time. She passed the test. It had taken her six years!

Patience allowed these people to keep moving on toward their dreams. Patience can help you to keep on moving toward your dream—toward becoming PRESIDENT OF YOUR LIFE!

CHAPTER 19

The Dream Killer

Now I want to tell you about a killer. It is something that kills hopes and dreams. It can kill the wishes you have. That killer is a *negative mental attitude.*

With a negative mental attitude, you can easily quit. You can give in to doubt and fear. A negative mental attitude assures you that you don't have what it takes. It tells you that you will fail. It tells you that you do not have the potential to achieve your goals. A negative mental attitude can make you an "impossibility thinker."

What happens when you fill your mind with negative attitudes and thoughts?

The negative emotions that come with these attitudes and thoughts are:

Worry	Tension
Despair	Guilt
Anger	Jealousy
Suspicion	Sorrow
Anxiety	Pessimism

You don't need these emotions! And you don't need a negative mental attitude.

What you want in the Cabinet of Your Presidency is the opposite—a *positive mental attitude.*

The positive emotions that come with this attitude are:

Hope	Determination
Trust	Self-respect
Courage	Ambition
Joy	Freedom
Confidence	Optimism

These are the emotions you want working for you. That is why you want to develop a *positive mental attitude.*

The attitude you take is up to you. Henry Ford, developer of the Ford automobile, once declared, "Think you can, think you can't—either way you'll be right."

You must begin thinking and knowing that *you can.* You must add a positive mental attitude to your cabinet.

Your positive mental attitude is to your life what horsepower is to an automobile. Low horsepower means low output, slow speed. The greater the horsepower of an engine, the higher the output, the faster the speed.

You want to have high output, you want to move down the road toward your goals. You want to develop a positive mental attitude. How do you do it? First of all, you say to yourself every day: "Today I'll make things happen. Today I will accomplish some of my goals."

You will put aside negative thoughts and pessimistic ideas each time they try to enter your mind. You will ignore people who have negative thoughts. You will not let the negative failures of others transform *you* into a loser.

I'm sure you see and hear negative thoughts all the time. Nearly every school, every factory, every business office has some people who are negative. They always find fault. They don't like the boss, they don't like the furniture, they wish their desk was on the other side of the room. And this type of person always makes fun of those who are working hard, who are trying to do their best.

Nine times out of ten, the person who is negative about others is really saying to us, "*I* can't achieve, *I* can't do anything, so I'm going to convince everyone that those who *can* do things are fools." Don't be taken in by it! Don't let that kind of person mold you into the negative failure that he or she is.

Studies about students who learn and students who don't learn show it is a fact that *those who think they will not learn do not*. On the other hand, *those who think they will learn do so*. A negative or a positive attitude—that makes the difference.

Henry Ford, a man who insisted on a positive attitude, once decided that his automobiles should have unbreakable glass. He called in all the young, inexperienced workers in his laboratories and told them what he wanted. He knew that if he asked the experienced workers, they would say, "It's impossible." So he told the young ones—the ones who didn't know it was impossible—to make unbreakable glass, and they made it in a short time. It was the attitude that made the difference.

Whenever I think about positive mental attitude, I am reminded of a man named Tandy Rice. Tandy Rice runs an agency that schedules singing and speaking celebrities for performances around the world. He once picked up a newspaper and read that another agency, not his, had signed former President Gerald Ford to a contract.

"Well," Tandy Rice said, "a craving was flung on me. My competitive juices started flowing." Tandy Rice set out that day to sign up a celebrity to match what the other agency was doing. The celebrity Tandy Rice set out to enlist was Billy Carter, the President's brother.

It was a tough task he had set for himself, Tandy Rice soon found. "It would have been easier to get to see the Pope," Tandy Rice said later. "At the peanut business, there were guards at the door. It looked like everybody in the country wanted to get a glimpse of Billy Carter."

Billy Carter changed his phone number often in order to discourage callers. And he seldom was seen outside his business offices.

Tandy Rice did some research. He found out that Billy Carter and he had two interests in common. One was business—"I found out he was a no-nonsense businessman"—and the other was that he loved country music.

So Tandy Rice sent Billy Carter a telegram that started out: "Dear Mr. Carter. Dolly Parton and Porter Wagoner asked me to write you."

The telegram got Billy Carter's attention. He contacted Tandy Rice. And the two businessmen soon were working together.

That is letting a positive mental attitude work for you.

And that won't be the end of his story. Tandy Rice has probably set another goal for himself—signing up Billy Carter's brother as a client of his agency when he leaves the White House. I wouldn't want to bet that he won't do it.

Let me tell you one more story about positive mental attitude. In a Viet Cong concentration camp there was an American prisoner of war who was a well-educated man. One day his fellow American prisoners noticed him practicing the art of barbering. They asked the reason that he was trying to learn barbering. He replied that a barber was the only one who was allowed in to see the other prisoners who were in solitary confinement.

"Why do you want to do that?" they asked. "Nobody is allowed to say a word to them when they enter their solitary cells."

"Yes, I know," he said, "but just maybe I will be able to encourage them."

Finally he learned to cut hair and was allowed to be the barber for the solitary prisoners. Always he was under heavy guard as he cut their hair to make sure that no words were passed. He would go in and begin cutting a prisoner's hair. And at least three times during the barbering he would say firmly, "Please, hold your chin up." The guards thought this comment was spoken just for the purpose of proper cutting.

And I say to you, "Please, hold your chin up." The next

time you are down, remember this story and hold *your* chin up. Keep your *positive mental attitude* up. Your mind can't hold two thoughts in the same space. The *dominant* thought you put into your mind is the one that will affect the thoughts and actions that come from your mind.

So be careful. Check your thoughts. Only *you* can put thought in your mind. Let your thoughts be positive. You want power—horsepower to make your life move. You want to become the person you can be. The power of a *positive mental attitude* is perhaps your greatest friend in helping you accomplish your goals. The power of a *positive mental attitude* can help you become PRESIDENT OF YOUR LIFE.

CHAPTER 20

Goals Mean "I Can"

This may seem hard to believe, but it is true: The main reason most people don't get what they want in life is that they *don't know what they want!*

Before people can accomplish what they want to accomplish, they must have in mind exactly what it is they want. Before *you* can become what you want in life, *you* must know exactly what you want to become.

You know this is true because you know about the Law of Cause and Effect. You know that what you think about is what you become.

That is why it is important—absolutely essential—that you put *Goals* into your Cabinet for the Presidency of Your Life.

So many people, young and old, do not know what they want. Ask most men or women what it is that they want and they will answer, "happiness," or "money," or "a good personality." But these things are all vague wishes. A goal must be specific, clear-cut.

All of us have dreams, wishes, ideas, hopes of what we would like to do, what we would like to become. But for most people that is what they remain—dreams, wishes, ideas, hopes.

The first step toward getting what you want is to decide and know *exactly* what it is that you want. Knowing this makes the difference.

Let me tell you about a man who knew this rule. He was not a well-educated man. He dropped out of school at age fourteen, never finishing the tenth grade. His family was poor; they were farmers, and as a boy he learned to pick cotton for $1.25 a hundred pounds.

But when he was four, an uncle gave him a guitar, a five-dollar bargain from the Sears catalog. That was all he needed to set his goal to become a top singing star.

He began by playing guitar in clubs and on the road, usually for little money. Later he played as a studio musician—playing back-up music for singers that all of us have heard of—Frank Sinatra, Dean Martin, Elvis Presley.

But he was an unknown. "None of the singing stars I backed ever even knew my name," he said. "I was just the guy on the end picking the guitar."

He was earning good money as a studio musician, but that wasn't his goal. So he quit and started singing and appearing on his own. It was risky, but it was what he had set as *his goal.*

He recorded "Gentle On My Mind" and then "By the Time I Get to Phoenix"—and the rest is music history. Glen Campbell reached his goal—he became the singing star he had envisioned. He was not the "overnight sensation" the newspapers said he was. He had been at it for twenty-five years. "I had tough times," he said, "but I always knew what I wanted to do." And that is what you must do if you are to become President of Your Life.

How do you start? You take your dream or wish and you reduce it to one clear-cut sentence.

You don't speculate, "I'd sort of like to get into the cleaning business." You say, "I will own the largest chain of cleaning stores in the city." You don't mention, "I'd like to go to college." You vow, "I will attend and graduate in the top 10 percent of the students at my state university." Then your wish becomes a thing you can accomplish. It becomes a destination—and like an airplane pilot, you don't take off until you know where you plan to land.

If you do not yet have a dream or a wish that is clear enough to make into a goal, try this: Imagine yourself five years from now. Ask yourself: What education do I want to have? What job training do I want to complete? What home life do I expect? What kind of house would I like to live in? How much money do I want to make? What kind of friends do I want to have?

Or try this: Each day for a week take ten minutes and list all the possible goals you might consider. At the end of the week you will have a list of dozens, maybe hundreds, of possible goals.

This exercise will force you to express your goals in writing. And that is an excellent way to begin to make your goals specific and clear-cut.

Remember, the important thing is not where you are and what you are *now*, or what you *have been*. The important thing is *where you will be five years from now, what you will be five years from now—or one week from now*. And that can be only if you set goals for yourself.

The greatest value of setting goals is that you stop wasting your time, stop aimless drifting. You no longer have to daydream. You know where you are going, so you can concentrate your efforts on getting there.

Goals will make you stronger. Goals will motivate you and give you ambition. Goals will give you the courage to try again when you fail. Goals will move you forward toward something. They give you a future. They keep you from going backward and worrying about the past. Goals give you an identity. "Who are you?" "I am a person who will have achieved this goal by this time."

Having goals means the beginnings of success. Not having goals can mean failure.

Suppose you really don't have any goals right now—or suppose you don't have *the big goal* yet.

Goal-setting is just as important for you, because sometime you will suddenly find your dream goal. If you set smaller goals for yourself now and practice achieving them, you will know how to go about it when your big goal comes along. You will be prepared.

If you still feel, as many others do, that you don't know what your goals are, I will let you in on a secret. *Anything you are doing today, you can do better than you did yesterday.* This gives you goals for every day of your life!

You can do a better job in school today than you did yesterday. You can do a better job in your work than you did yesterday. You can get along better with others today than you did yesterday. You can do a better job today of putting your religion into practice than you did yesterday. These are wonderful goals—meaningful goals that can bring results.

Another excellent starting point for setting goals for yourself is to sit down and think about these questions:

"What is the person that I want to be like?"

"How does that person that I want to become conduct himself or herself spiritually?"

"How does the person I want to become act as a worker, a student, a friend?"

After you have thought these questions through—when you can see in your mind's eye that person you want to be—then write it down. Stick it on a mirror in your room and read it twice each day.

Set one goal for each area of your life—your work life, your school life, your life relating to others, your spiritual life.

Set one goal at a time. Work at it, and when you have succeeded at it, set another, and another. Become the person you dream of being.

Goals say, "I can; I will." Goals say, "I believe in the Law of Cause and Effect, and I am applying it every day in my life." Goals say, "I am directing my future." Goals will help you become PRESIDENT OF YOUR LIFE!

CHAPTER 21

Confidence Builds Respect

The final member of Your Cabinet for the Presidency of Your Life is *self-confidence.* This means having the wisdom to respect yourself—to realize that you are one of the greatest productions God has made.

Dwight D. Eisenhower—President of the United States, a great general, and an honored soldier—was once asked what was the most important aspect of life to him. He answered, "After all, the most important thing is one's self-respect."

"One's self-respect!" To realize that you are an individual with just as much potential as any in the world. And remember what we learned many pages back. Most of us are using just 10 percent of our potential! Think how much more you can be now that you are making plans to use more and more of your potential.

How do you increase your self-confidence, your respect for yourself? One salesman of whom I know helped himself grow by writing a commercial about himself. He wrote it down on a piece of paper and glued it to his mirror. Every morning as be began to shave, he read the commercial. It said, "You are one of the most talented men in the world. You have achieved many things. You are going to achieve many more. How great to be you!"

This salesman remembered what others may have forgotten. We have to sell every product, every idea, over and over again. Coca-Cola would soon drop from sight in the stores if someone didn't keep reminding people over and over that it is a great soft drink.

If this is true of a soft drink, how much more true is it of a developing human personality—you? Unlike a commercial product, you can grow, learn, and accomplish. Perhaps you should sell yourself to your most important customer—yourself! Sell yourself on the idea that you have great reserves of inner potential, because you do. Sell yourself on the idea that you have untapped talents and skills, because you do. Dare yourself to turn your dreams into goals, because you can.

So often we all give up too soon. We fail to keep trying. And so often the reasons we don't try are completely false. We say, "It's impossible" or "Well, *I* can't do it." Or "I can't change." But we can.

Are you familiar with the story of the pike and the minnows? A pike is a fish that loves to eat minnows. As an experiment, a man put some pike in a large tank of water divided in half by a glass pane. On the other side of the pane were minnows.

At first, the pike raced toward the minnows to eat them. But, of course, the pike bumped into the glass divider and could not get to the minnows. Soon the pike didn't even bother bumping against the glass. They gave up.

Even more amazing, when the experimenter *removed* the glass divider, the pike didn't even try to catch the minnows! The pike had learned to fail! They had lost their confidence in even trying to catch minnows.

Don't be like the pike. Keep trying. Many times you

will find that the glass divider keeping you from your goal isn't even there. It was removed long ago, and if you just try, you will succeed.

Another excuse used by some people is that because they have failed once or twice, they can never succeed now.

This is humbug. Example after example after example shows that failing a few times doesn't mean failing later. We have already read about many examples of this truism: Abraham Lincoln, Lucille Ball, O.J. Simpson, Jim Irwin, and others. Allow me to mention a few more:

Woody Allen—flunked motion picture production at two colleges;

Malcolm Forbes, editor-in-chief of *Forbes* magazine—did not make the staff of his school newspaper at Princeton;

Author Leon Uris—flunked high school English three times;

Actress Liv Ullman—failed an audition for the state theater school in Norway when the judges said she had no talent;

Irving Berlin—told by a famous music director, "You'll never find anyone interested in your 'Alexander's Ragtime Band' ";

Novelist Charlotte Brontë—told by William Wordsworth, England's poet laureate, that she wrote like "a notary's clerk or a demented seamstress."

I could go on and on with these examples, but you see the point. Almost everyone who has succeeded has been considered a failure at one time. The difference between them and the persons who failed is that they did not give up. They know—as you know—that each human being has talent within him. They knew—as you know—that all of us can succeed *if we keep trying*. They had self-confidence. They believed in themselves. You, too, can build self-confidence. You can believe in yourself and in your dream. You can put action behind your beliefs.

God in His wisdom might have made somebody finer to

be President of Your Life. But He didn't. He made you that President.

You are somebody.

You are PRESIDENT OF YOUR LIFE.

CHAPTER 22

Presidential Powers

Up to this point, you have learned about the powers that can help you achieve what you want in your life—the powers of your Presidency.

You know about the "Acres of Diamonds" within yourself.

You know that you have a *free choice* to do what you want with your life.

You know about the *Law of Cause and Effect*, and you know that what you want to *happen* you must first *think*.

You have learned the importance of *believing in yourself* and in what you can do.

You know, too, that actions of the mind can build *habits* that will help you.

You know about the power of *affirmation*—the power to decide now to do more, to be more, each day.

You have learned to *picture in your mind* the things you want to have and the things you want to achieve.

And, you know about the *Law of Spiritual Power* that can put God on your side.

You have learned, too, that there are enemies of your

Presidency. Enemies that cause you to say "I can't," "What if I fail?" and "It's impossible."

You know also that you have a cabinet of friends to help you overcome these enemies. A cabinet filled with En- thusiasm, Action, the Golden Rule, Patience, a Positive Mental Attitude, Goals, and Self-Confidence.

At the conclusion of this book, I am leaving you a suggested plan to use in establishing this Cabinet—to make these friends work for you day by day, week by week.

First, however, I want to tell you about a formula for changing your life, for making your dreams come true, for success. If you follow this formula, made up of four steps, you will be guaranteed to become PRESIDENT OF YOUR LIFE!

CHAPTER 23

You *Can* Change

One United States President had a sign on his desk. It read: "The Buck Stops Here."

When you decide to change your life—to achieve, to grow—you must keep this sign in mind. For it is true, "The buck stops here." It stops with you. *You* and *you alone* can take the steps that will change *your* life.

I cannot do it for you. Neither your parents, your husband or your wife can do it for you. Your teachers, friends—no one else can make that decision for you.

If you want to change, to move forward, *you* must decide to take the initiative. It may be one of the most difficult tasks you have ever done in your life. Because change is the one thing we all hate to do. We are comfortable with our old ideas, our old habits, our old choices. It makes no difference that they are weak ideas, bad habits, poor choices—they are the ideas, habits, and choices with which we are most comfortable.

We know what happens with these old ideas, habits, and choices. If we let them alone, they will save us lots of work.

They will manipulate our lives for us. They will save us the trouble of becoming presidents of our lives.

But is that what *you* want? I don't think so. I don't think you would be reading this book if you did not want to change, if you did not want to become SOMEBODY.

As you learned earlier, most of us use only 10 percent of our ability during our lifetimes. With 10 percent of your ability, you probably can get along. You can usually get through school, hold down a job, get by. Is that what you want? If you do, you know that you can have it. You know about the Law of Free Choice. If you *choose* to use just 10 percent of yourself you will *do so*. But you also have the free choice to do more—and to be more.

Why, then, do many of us remain 10 percenters? Why do we not at least become 20 percenters, becoming twice the person we are?

Why? Because to extract more potential, to do more, to be more, to become the person we want to become can happen only if we *change*. We must change our thoughts, our beliefs, our habits, our actions.

We run from change. We run because to change means *doing*, not *wishing*. To change means work, patience, energy, time. It means we have to face the unknown.

So we allow life to go on, and we complain about the way things are. We say that we want them to be different and better, while we do nothing to make that change come about.

But let me assure you of this. *We can change.* Think of people you know who have changed. Think of the fat person who went on a diet and got thin. Think of the student who failed but came back and passed. Think of the people you know who earned good grades, won games, got good jobs. Think of the people who turned sour marriages into happy marriages.

I am sure you can think of many examples among people you have met. Let me tell you about one woman who changed her life from nothing to something great. Her name is Mary C. Crowley. When she was eighteen months old, her mother died of pneumonia. Young Mary was sent to live with her grandmother on a farm. Even before she was five, she had to help with the farm chores, clean, and wash dishes.

Meanwhile, her father remarried and decided to bring his children back together. This decision began another sad chapter in Mary Crowley's life. It turned out that her father's new wife was a cruel woman who mistreated the children. Finally, a court ruled that she was an unfit mother. Mary was again sent to live with her grandparents.

She lived a lonely childhood, but finished high school ahead of the other young men and women her age. Because she was lonely, she got married very young. The marriage didn't last and soon Mary Crowley found herslf alone with two small children to support. She found a job, but it was barely enough to support her family.

At this point, Mary Crowley made a decision. Would she remain a nobody, struggling to bring up children, scraping for every penny? Or would she be more, would she become President of Her Life?

She decided to change, to grow—to become something more than she was. She started taking accounting classes. She got a better job, worked all day, and took classes at Southern Methodist University at night. She worked on weekends, too, and spent time with her children.

Mary Crowley had an interst in home decoration, and she decided to build on her interest. She quit her accounting job and started to sell consumer products at parties held in her home. Next, she joined a home accessories importing company. Then, she created her own company—Home Interiors and Gifts, Inc.

That was in 1957. Today, Mary Crowley's company has 23,000 sales representatives working in 49 states. In addition, she counsels and trains other women for business life. Needless to say, her income is sufficient to care for her needs and for her family.

She is a speaker eagerly sought by groups of all kinds. She serves on several boards of directors and became the first woman member of the Dallas Chamber of Commerce.

Mary Crowley made the decision to change her life. In her words, "I wanted to be somebody. and I believe that God never takes time to make a nobody." If Mary Crowley can change her life, so can you. If others can change their lives, so can you. After all, you have 90 percent of your potential still inside waiting to be used! You can begin to mine your diamonds. You can change. I'll tell you how.

CHAPTER 24

A Burning Desire

The beginning point for change is the *desire to change.*
You must really want to change.

I don't mean just a passing wish for change. I mean a
burning, consuming, strong desire to have things different
in your life. You must have a burning desire to earn better
grades, to treat others better, to become better at something
that is important to you. You must have a burning desire to
become the person you want to be socially, spiritually, and
in your school or work. You must have the kind of desire
the Mary Crowley had—a desire strong enough to make you
begin to change, as she did. You must have the kind of
"purple passion" that Carol Channing had when she
pushed to make "Hello Dolly" the top musical hit in the
nation. You must have a burning desire as strong as Johnny
Cash's wish was while he locked himself in his bedroom to
go "cold turkey" off drugs.

You *can* build that kind of desire. You can build it by
thinking of what in your life you are dissatisfied with, what
habits you want to change, what makes you feel unhappy
and inferior. Then, start imagining how you will feel when

you overcome those bad habits, make improvements, earn more money, win more friends, get a better job—become the person you can be.

Virginia Wade is a tennis player who won at Wimbledon—but only after she learned how important it was to *really* want to win. Virginia Wade was an excellent tennis player in college, easily winning college championships. When she had a chance to go to Wimbledon, even though it was at examination time, she accepted. "It never occurred to me that I couldn't handle it," she said. And she couldn't. Trying to study and play tennis at the same time didn't work, she discovered. Winning required much more than just going out and playing, she learned.

As a result, year after year, Virginia Wade played well but never won the big tournaments. "I relied too much on a great afternoon's luck," she said.

And luck will not always bring us through to victory. It takes more. It takes concentrated desire focused on a goal.

Virginia Wade did everything she was supposed to do. She practiced hard and long, and she spent years learning tennis techniques. But she still was not winning the big ones.

Then she found out the reason. "There's a big difference between passively *wishing* and actively *wanting*," she now says. "If you waste time wishing, you can't be alert to any of the practical solutions marching by you."

Once she learned this lesson—the need to have a burning desire—Virginia Wade began to win. Her practice began to pay off. And at age thirty-two, eleven years after she had set out to do it, she won at Wimbledon.

What made the difference? The difference was that her hope and wish to win was replaced by a *burning desire* to win. Then she was able to change her life.

You can change your life, as Virginia Wade did. You know *now* what it took her *years* to learn—that a burning desire can ignite change. Start now to change your life. Start now to build a burning desire for your goals.

CHAPTER 25

A Specific Goal

You now know that to change your life you must begin by building desire. But having a burning desire is not enough. You must turn that desire into a *goal*. This means that you must have in mind a specific, clear-cut goal. You must picture it in your mind until you can see a sharp picture of exactly what you want your goal to be.

For example, if you want to change so you can earn better grades in school, you must set the exact goal of what you want—not a vague, "I'd like to pass more courses," or "I'd like to receive better grades." Your desire must become a specific goal. "I must pass four out of five courses this semester," or "I must earn at least two A's and two B's this semester."

If your goal is a better job, you must picture a *specific* job you want and say to yourself exactly *when* you want to get that job. You cannot say to yourself, "I'd like a better job— maybe in selling." You must be specific. You must say, "I want a better job. That job will be in selling. I want to sell a specific kind of product. I will begin my search for that job by talking with Jim Smith, who is a salesman in that field. Then I will write letters to seven companies which hire salesmen. I will follow up each of those letters one week later with a phone call to the person I wrote to, and I will ask him or her for an interview."

If your goal is a better marriage, you must picture *exactly* how you want your marriage to improve. You must picture the improved marriage as you want it—the kind of conversations you want to have with your wife or husband, the kind of actions you will take to make changes, the kind of activities in which you and your spouse will jointly participate. And you must tell yourself exactly when you will begin those conversations, those actions for change.

Not many years ago, actor Richard Burton found out how important it is to have a specific goal. Richard Burton is a successful actor. But he had a failing and he knew it. He was misusing alcohol to the point where it was ruining his life.

Several of Richard Burton's friends had met the same enemy. One of them, actor Peter O'Toole, had stopped drinking after his doctors told him he had a choice: Go dry or end up in a mortuary.

Richard Burton made his decision to change after he had starred in the film, *The Clansman.* He realized that he had been drinking so much he had no memory of working on the picture! "I'd like to meet some of the actors I worked with in that film," he said. "I understand they are wonderful people, but I can't recall a single scene."

This frightening experience helped Richard Burton form a *burning desire* to change his life. And next he set a *specific goal* for himself. That goal was total sobriety—an unclouded life without alcohol. He imagined exactly what he wanted, even imagined what he would lose in companionship with drinking friends. He knew he had to change the habits of a lifetime. He knew he could do it if he had a specific goal.

Richard Burton began a program of physical therapy, swimming each day and jogging. He eliminated alcohol from his life.

It took two years of his life to reach this goal, but he succeeded. Now he gives thanks for the new life which his goal has brought him. Remarried and sober, Richard Burton says, "I've enjoyed a resurgence of work. I find I move much faster than during my drinking days, and my mind works quicker."

Richard Burton translated his desire for change into a specific goal. *You* must take *your* burning desires and change them into specific goals for *your* life. You *can* do it. Start immediately. Write the *exact goals* you have. Then you will have taken another step on the way toward changing your life—toward becoming **PRESIDENT OF YOUR LIFE.**

CHAPTER 26

Write It Down

You are learning how to change your life. You know that in order to change you must have a *burning desire*; you know that you must *make that desire into a clear-cut goal.*

Once you have gone this far—once you have spelled out your goals—you are already ahead of most people in this world. It is estimated that only 10 percent of all people have taken the trouble to spell out their goals by actually writing them down. You are now among those 10 percent!

But even this action is not sufficient if you are to change your life, if you are to overcome feelings of inferiority, if you are to become somebody. You must also *draw up a plan for making your goals come true.*

The reason that many goals don't become reality is not because they are poor or unworthy goals. It is because the person who had the goals did not devise a plan to meet them.

If I were to offer you $20,000 if you could drive from Miami, Florida, to Los Angeles, California, and return in twelve days, the first thing you would do in accepting my offer would be to get a good road map and begin to mark your route. You would mark the road you would travel each day, and you would compute the distance you would have to drive.

If you were to build a house, you would begin with a blueprint—a specific plan showing exactly what the house was to look like, the size of each room, the location of each window.

So if you want to carry out the goals for building your life—for taking you from this point to your goal—then *you must look at some maps and draw a set of blueprints.*

Goals will never be achieved unless the steps for reaching them are deliberately and thoughtfully planned.

Your personal plan must tell you *exactly how* you will accomplish your goal. It must spell out, *step by step*, what you will do, what you will stop doing, how much time you will spend doing it—the price you will pay to achieve your goal.

For example, if your goal is to get a better job, your plan must tell you *where* you will look for that job; *when* you will learn the skills that job needs; to whom you will talk about the job you want; *what* you will sacrifice so you have time to learn about and seek the new job.

Your goal must be specific, it must be step by step, and it must include exact time limits.

Let's look at an example of how one person might devise a plan for a new job. Let's suppose this person has a high school degree and has worked for two years as a mechanic's assistant in a small auto repair shop. He has a burning desire to improve himself. He has set as his specific goal becoming a class A mechanic with his city's bus company.

Now he begins to outline his plan. It might look like this.

My goal: getting a new job.

My specific goal: getting a new job as a mechanic with the city bus company.

My specific goal with time limits: getting a new job as a mechanic with the city bus company within sixty days.

How I will accomplish this goal:

Step one: I will find out more information about the bus company—about who does the hiring; who is the man to whom he reports; how many job vacancies they have; what pay they offer beginning mechanics; what training they expect of beginners.

How: I will talk with John Gorman, a man with whom I went to school who works for the bus company.

When: I will call him today and talk with him in person before the week is out.

Step two: I will seek an interview with the bus company's employment manager.

How: I will ask John Gorman to allow me to use his name as someone recommending me. Then I will call the employment manager and press him for an interview appointment. I will politely request an interview, even if he says they are not now hiring beginning mechanics.

When: I will call him the day after I talk with John Gorman.

Step three: I will prepare for my employment interview.

How: First, I will check out a book from the public library that tells about employment interviews, how to dress for them, and how to deal with them. Second, I will call Mr. Jenkins, who was my high school counselor, and ask him to talk with me about employment interviews. Third, I will study the information I have gotten from John Gorman so I know as much about the bus company as possible before the interview.

When: I will check the book out today and call Mr. Jenkins today.

Step four: I will have the employment interview.

And so on. This man's plan will also tell exactly what he will do if he does *not* get a job on the first try. It may call for his enrolling in additional training courses. It may be necessary for him to change his timetable and to reapply after more training or after the company expands.

The important thing is that the plan tells him exactly *what* he must do and exactly *when* he must do it. The better his plan, the better his chance of completing it, the better his chance, in this case, of getting the job he wants.

This same type of plan will work for a secretary seeking a better paying office job, a student seeking his first full-time job, or an experienced business man or woman looking for a more advanced position. You can make a specific plan like this one for any goal you have in your mind.

Try it now. Begin to write down the exact steps *you* will take to bring *your dream* closer to you.

Making plans—and carrying them out—is what will make you different from the others in this world who never plan, who just wish.

Making your plans and executing them will make you PRESIDENT OF YOUR LIFE.

CHAPTER 27

See It Through

Change means a burning desire, turning that desire into a goal, and building a plan to reach that goal.

But even this isn't sufficient. You need to do one more task to bring about change in your life. The final and perhaps the most difficult part is *committing your goal and plan to action.*

It is great to dream of a goal and to desire to achieve it. It's fine to outline a plan. But all this effort will come to no end if you do not decide *now* that you *will not quit.* You must decide to keep on keeping on until you have completed the plan and reached the goal. You must decide if you are willing to put forth all the self-discipline that commitment requires.

This attitude involves knowing in advance that you may fail the first time or the second time—or the tenth time you try. But you must commit yourself *now* to continue toward your goal even if things seem to go wrong or if you seem to be making little progress. Always keep that goal as the picture in your mind's eye.

This is sometimes called determination or perseverance.

It means "sticking to it." Mostly it is hard work and determined effort. But if this hard work—this commitment—is *not* made, all your bright desires and hopeful goals will fail.

Why? Because it is human nature to begin a project bursting with enthusiasm, spending a lot of energy. But pretty soon we tire. We have something else we want to do. Some sweat will break out, and we don't want to pay the price to carry through on our plans.

You can tell when a person gets to this point. He begins to blame everyone and everything but himself for the failure. "Bad luck," he will cry. Or, "I didn't have the time I needed." Or, "This wasn't the year for that kind of business."

That, instead of saying that our dream didn't come true because we failed to commit ourselves to the work, effort, and necessary time.

Winners are able to achieve because they always keep the picture of their goal, their dream, in the front of their minds. The dream is more important than anything else. Winners persist; they hang on.

Commitment to a goal means:

●Being willing to work at it one step at a time;

●Not thinking about all the work that will come tomorrow, but instead *doing* what must be done today;

●Putting off today's pleasures for greater rewards tomorrow;

●Keeping the goal in mind;

Napoleon Hill, the great writer and speaker, once said, "Great people are just ordinary people with an extra amount of determination."

You can build this extra amount of determination. You can stick to it.

YOU *can* do it!

Remember this: There is no other way to change. Luck won't do it. Someone else won't do it for you. It can't be done easily, but it *can* be done. You can change your life; you can direct your future—if you use this formula:

First, create in yourself a burning desire to change.

Second, make that desire into a clear-cut goal.

Third, develop a plan for making the goal come true.

Fourth, commit yourself to the actions needed to bring about your goal.

It takes much courage to begin to change. It takes courage to change old habits, old thoughts, old actions. It takes conscious effort and hard work. It takes patience and determination.

But you *can* do it! You can become PRESIDENT OF YOUR LIFE!

CHAPTER 28

The Decision Is Yours

You now have in your hands and in your mind all the tools you need to become **PRESIDENT OF YOUR LIFE.**

You need no longer feel inferior.

You need no longer be a nobody.

You have the tools to become the somebody you want to be.

You have the tools to become the student you want to be, the worker you want to be, the family member you want to be, the spiritual person you want to be.

You can be successful. Just start mining your diamonds.

You can be great. Just go back and dig deeper—mine more of your diamonds.

Today is *your* day.

You can begin today to dream dreams for yourself that never were.

You can say "I can" and "I will."

Or you can turn away and always wonder about what might have been—about the person *you* might have been.

The decision is yours.

You are the **PRESIDENT OF YOUR LIFE!**

And so I will leave you now, but in good hands . . .
YOURS.
There at YOUR WHITE HOUSE.

A Seven-Week Plan

"Knowing is not enough. We must apply. Willing is not enough. We must do."

—Goethe

You have now learned about the power you have to change your life—to start becoming PRESIDENT OF YOUR LIFE.

This final part of the book is a seven-week program to help you maintain a strong presidency by building up the cabinet of friends that can help you attain your goals.

You remember that these cabinet friends are:

Enthusiasm

Action

The Golden Rule

Patience

A Positive Mental Attitude

Goals

Self-Confidence

If you want to bring positive change into your life, begin to "do it now" by following these instructions. If you follow these instructions exactly, you will soon begin to notice changes in your life.

Don't be surprised to find that others are noticing, too, and commenting on "the new you."

Expect your life to take on positive purpose, direction, and fulfillment. Expect these things to happen *more and more* as you put *more and more* effort into this program.

Here are the instructions for your seven-week program— a program that will start you on the road to becoming PRESIDENT OF YOUR LIFE.

1. You will work with each of the following pages for five days (Monday through Friday). Each Monday morning you will begin with a new page for the week. (Begin with Number 1 and continue in numerical order through Number 7.)

2. Read the page three times per day—before work or school, at lunch, and at bedtime.

3. Practice what the page says throughout the day.

4. After the reading at bedtime, grade yourself for that day.

5. Do this for seven weeks (a new page each week). When you have finished Number 7, begin the process over with Number 1.

6. EXPECT RESULTS—WATCH YOURSELF GROW!

FIRST WEEK: ENTHUSIASM

Today, this world, my world, will be a better world because one person—ME—has given to everything I do and everyone I am around my ENTHUSIASM. I have this enthusiasm to give because of my strong belief in the purposes of my world, my work, my goals, and the good that exists in every person.

This belief causes me to have energy, excitement, and self-confidence. Enthusiasm causes me to put action behind my belief. I am, therefore, able to keep on keeping on, not to give up, to do my best. Enthusiasm will make me a winner.

TODAY, I will show this enthusiasm by smiling at each person I meet. This will say to them, "You Are Somebody." Not smiling at them may leave them feeling that they are a nobody, that they're not important.

TODAY, I will be cheerful and positive—not sour and negative—in my thoughts, my actions, and my reactions towards all people and all situations.

TODAY, by putting ENTHUSIASM (positive beliefs backed by actions) into all my work tasks, the tasks will be less difficult, and I will do a better job of everything I do today than I did yesterday.

TODAY, because I practice ENTHUSIASM, I will be happy.

* * *

I read this ENTHUSIASM page three times today, thought about its message, and practiced what it said to do in my daily living.

I rate my efforts for today with a score of:

M	T	W	T	F

1—lowest 2—poor 3—average 4—good 5—highest

SECOND WEEK: ACTION

Today will be a successful day for me because I will not put off doing the things I should do. I will "DO IT NOW."

By postponing tasks, I will increase my worries; I will begin to dread what I should do and not want to do it; and I will begin to feel burdened down. But postponing tasks will most often lead to my not doing them.

Success is possible only by doing. Therefore, today will be successful for me because I will "DO IT NOW."

Today I will get much work accomplished, because I will "DO IT NOW."

Today I will do something kind I have been wanting to do for someone and haven't, and I will "DO IT NOW."

Today I will do a better job of everything I do than I did yesterday, and I will "DO IT NOW."

If I practice the habit of "DO IT NOW," today will be a successful day for me . . . and so will tomorrow.

* * *

I read this ACTION page three times today, thought about its message, and practiced what it said to do in my daily living.

I rate my efforts for today with a score of:

M	T	W	T	F

1—lowest 2—poor 3—average 4—good 5—highest

THIRD WEEK: GOLDEN RULE

Happiness will be my partner all day long today because I will live by the Golden Rule. I will treat each person in the way I would like to be treated. Other people's feelings and happiness will be more important to me today than mine.

I will think only positive thoughts toward each person I meet. I will think of their good points, rather than their bad, because I know nobody is perfect—not even me.

I will pay honest compliments to others because everyone wants to be appreciated and feel needed by others.

I will not criticize someone else and thereby try to make myself look superior or important.

I will give kindness and consideration and respect to each person I meet today. I will keep these gifts a secret, for they are not a gift if I seek in return a reward or payment or applause.

Today I will live by the Golden Rule . . . I will do unto others as I would have them do unto me.

***

I read this GOLDEN RULE page three times today, thought about its message, and practiced what it said to do in my daily living.

I rate my efforts for today with a score of:

M	T	W	T	F

1—lowest 2—poor 3—average 4—good 5—highest

FOURTH WEEK: PATIENCE

Because I am not PATIENT, because I do not keep on keeping on, because I quit and give up when I become tired or discouraged—for these reasons I do not accomplish the things I want to accomplish; I do not become the person I want to become.

PATIENCE teaches me to keep going no matter how many times I fail or get frustrated and discouraged trying to reach my goal. Having my goal come true will be more important than how long it takes or how much failure and discouragement I experience before success is mine.

I will not try to turn today into tomorrow or the next day. Today is what I have been given, so I will live today.

PATIENCE will allow me to do only one thing at a time. PATIENCE will keep me from doing several things at once and becoming nervous, worried, tense, and rude towards others. PATIENCE will enable me to complete one task and then begin another.

I will not become discouraged, I am not a quitter, I am not rude. If I am tempted, I will take one more step, try one more time.

I will be PATIENT . . . I will PERSIST . . . I will succeed.

***

I read this PATIENCE page three times today, thought about its message, and practiced what it said to do in my daily living.

I rate my efforts for today with a score of:

M	T	W	T	F

1—lowest 2—poor 3—average 4—good 5—highest

FIFTH WEEK: POSITIVE MENTAL ATITUDE

My thoughts are one aspect of my life over which I have absolute control. This fact means that I have free choice over what thoughts I allow to enter my mind. But, I know that whatever thoughts I allow into my mind will all come back out in the form of my actions, my attitudes, and my feelings toward others and toward myself.

Only good actions, only good attitudes, only good feelings will be mine today, because I will put only positive and good thoughts into my mind. This POSITIVE MENTAL ATTITUDE will allow me to find positive solutions to all situations with which I am faced.

Today I will not make excuses. I will not be negative.

Today I will pay strict attention to avoid thinking and saying negative words such as "can't," "impossible," "won't work," "I don't have what it takes," "out of the question," "hopeless," and "what if," for they keep me from acting and finding solutions.

Today will be a GOOD day . . . I will make it a GOOD day . . . I will keep a POSITIVE MENTAL ATTITUDE.

***

I read this POSITIVE MENTAL ATTITUDE page three times today, thought about its message, and practiced what it said to do in my daily living.

I rate my efforts for today with a score of:

M	T	W	T	F

1—lowest 2—poor 3—average 4—good 5—highest

SIXTH WEEK: GOALS

I will give direction, purpose, and meaning to my life today. I will accomplish this mission by setting goals for my actions, my attitudes, and my work. These goals will tell me what I am going to accomplish today.

I will develop a plan of action to accompany each goal. This plan of action will be the road map that tells me what I will do, when I will do it, and how I will do it so that each goal I have set will be reached.

I will attack the most difficult and demanding goals, or the ones I dread doing the most FIRST.

I will not quit until I have accomplished all the goals I have set for myself today. I may tire, I may get discouraged, I may not succeed on the first or second or third try, but I will not quit. I will accomplish my goals for today.

And when today is over, I will have known happiness and fulfillment because I gave my life direction and purpose and meaning . . . I set my GOALS . . . I accomplished my GOALS.

***

I read this GOALS page three times today, thought about its message, and practiced what it said to do in my daily living.

I rate my efforts for today with a score of:

M	T	W	T	F

1—lowest 2—poor 3—average 4—good 5—highest

SEVENTH WEEK: I AM SOMEBODY

Today I am not afraid; I feel confident toward myself and what I can accomplish. I am a president: president of my thoughts, president of my actions, president of my reactions, and president of the quality of my work—I am PRESIDENT OF MY LIFE.

As president, I am free to carry out any type of administration I wish—good, average, poor. However, I know that what I give to my administration determines what life gives me in return—not luck or fate. Whatever my action, I can expect the same type of reaction from the world in return.

In the past, I have been like the average person and used only 10 percent of my potential and ability; 90 percent of what I can be and do is still inside me begging to be used!

Today I will handle well all the situations that I face because I will use more of the untapped potential and ability that I possess.

I AM SOMEBODY . . . I am the PRESIDENT OF MY LIFE. Mine will be a good administration. I have potential! I have ability!

***

I have read this I AM SOMEBODY page three times today, thought about its message, and practiced what it said to do in my daily living.

I rate my efforts for today with a score of:

M	T	W	T	F

1—lowest 2—poor 3—average 4—good 5—highest